THE GRIP OF MONEY

WHY MONEY AND WORK STILL MASTER CHRISTIANS

JAMES JY KIM

The Grip of Money: Why Money and Work Still Master Christians

Cover illustration by Judy Lai.

Published by Gooby Publishing House

First published 2026

Printed in Australia

Formatted with Vellum

CONTENTS

For my brothers and sisters

Let go and live

ACKNOWLEDGEMENTS

To God — who always gave me a choice whether to work in ministry or in the marketplace. I never planned that the two worlds would converge in a book like this.

To HOME Church — This book would not exist without the sabbatical that you gave me. You sent me away trusting that the rest would be good for me. I hope it pays dividends to you as I present this to you. The heavy lifting of this manuscript happened in that season of rest, which feels entirely appropriate for a book about the Sabbath. Thank you for all the ways you model the principles in this book and for proving their truth by the fruit I see in your lives.

To my children — every benefit you enjoy living in our home and every peace you know is because mum and dad have tried to live out these principles in obedience and love towards Jesus. Money is a servant and not a master in our home. I pray that in time it will be the same in yours.

To my wife — thank you for saying yes three times. Yes to marriage. Yes to tithing. Yes to sabbatical at whatever the cost. When I told you I felt I needed to step back from a full time job as we were expecting our second child, you said: "You need it. God will provide." You were right. As always (almost).

A NOTE TO THE READER

The content of this book reflects the personal convictions, pastoral experience, and Biblical understanding of the author. It is intended for general encouragement and spiritual formation.

Nothing in this book constitutes financial, legal, investment, tax, or medical advice. The author is not a licensed financial adviser, legal practitioner, or medical professional. Before making any financial, legal, or medical decisions, readers should seek advice from a suitably qualified professional.

All personal stories and illustrations are drawn from the author's own experience or are used with permission. Where stories involve other individuals, identifying details have been changed or omitted to protect privacy. Any resemblance to specific persons beyond those intended is unintentional.

PREFACE

This is not an economics textbook, nor is it a self-help book on how to make money. These are my insights from twenty years of working in the church and in the marketplace — reflections as a preacher and as a practitioner.

The economic jargon is intentional, not to show off vocabulary, but to expose you to words you will hear in the public domain — on YouTube, in the news, and between people with an interest in money. The scriptural references are not proof texts of the principles, but rather to show that the Bible is hardly silent on these topics. And I have added my own stories throughout to illustrate that I'm learning too.

Neither work nor money should be our master. There is to be only one master in our lives: the Lord Jesus Christ. He alone is worthy of all our affection, our attention, and our devotion — money and work are just tools and mediums through which we express our loyalty to him. Jesus must be Lord: the master, the king, the highest authority. If he is not, then we will take his place on the throne, or money will, or work will — none of which make good masters.

The goal of money and work is neither to be debt-free nor financially free. It is to be "love of money" free. This book aims not to make you fall in love with making money or even fall in love with giving it away. It aims to point you towards the hard and narrow way that leads to life where money and work serve you and not the other way around.

For freedom Christ has set us free; stand firm therefore, and do not submit again to a yoke of slavery.
(Galatians 5:1)

PART ONE
MONEY

CHAPTER 1
WHAT MONEY ACTUALLY IS

THE ILLUSION OF CONTROL

Money is a medium of exchange. Its primary purpose is to facilitate trade. Without money, trade requires a double coincidence of wants. If I have apples and want oranges, I need to find someone who has oranges and wants apples and is willing to trade at the same moment. Money solves this. It makes trade efficient. It allows the exchange of goods and services without every transaction being a direct swap.

The reason money is so desirable is because money gives you power — purchasing power. Even a little extra money means more choice. More choice means more control over your diet, your housing, your leisure, your lifestyle. **The lure of money is ultimately the desire for more control.** But the desire for more control is in direct opposition to God's desire for you to give him control. This is why Jesus states that we cannot serve both God and money (Matthew 6:24) — they pull in opposite directions.

Sadly, wanting to control your life will end the same way it did for the rich young ruler who walked away from Jesus. The rich young ruler was not a bad person — he kept all the commandments (Mark 10:20); by every outward measure he was a "good person." But there was something holding him back from God and God's kingdom: it was his riches. His riches allowed him control, and giving away everything meant loss of control; even worse, it meant handing over control to someone else — namely Jesus. Mark records what happened next: *"Disheartened by the saying, he went away sorrowful, for he had great possessions"* (Mark 10:22).

The rich young ruler had a choice: **stay in control with riches or surrender control to Jesus.** This is a choice every person faces every day.

Control has the greatest grip on any person's life. Everyone wants it because everyone knows, deep inside, they do not have it. Jesus told a parable about a man who came into considerable wealth and thought his money had secured his future:

> "The land of a rich man produced plentifully, and he thought to himself, 'What shall I do, for I have nowhere to store my crops?' And he said, "I will do this: I will tear down my barns and build larger ones, and there I will store all my grain and my goods. And I will say to my soul, 'Soul, you have ample goods laid up for many years; relax, eat, drink, be merry.'" But God said to him, 'Fool! This night your soul is required of you, and the things you have prepared, whose will they be?' So is the one who lays up treasure for himself and is not rich toward God." *(Luke 12:16–21)*

He thought he was in control. He wasn't. **We are never truly in control.**

Nobody controls the future. This unsettling truth motivates most of us to find things that give a sense of control: insurance, savings, home ownership. But even with the best insurance, more savings than you need, and a fully paid-off house, nothing brings real security. There is still the body — the risk of cancer, neurological degeneration, metabolic dysfunction. There are still relationships, which no amount of money can control. There is still the spiritual — the question of purpose, meaning, peace.

This is why people love money: it gives the illusion that it can solve life's problems. And in some areas it helps — with better food and lifestyle, with building memories with loved ones. But none of these things are of any worth if they take you away from God. Unless God remains the centre and money is a tool, money will become your god.

THE PURSUIT

Your pursuit of God must be greater than your pursuit of money. **But the desire for more money will not end unless you decide to end it.** Having more money will appear to make your life better — and in many cases, it will — but the desire for more will ultimately outpace your ability to enjoy it, because there is no real enjoyment without God.

Solomon was arguably the wealthiest person in human history. He had everything he desired and was given everything he could not purchase himself. During his leadership, the entire kingdom of Israel was wealthy. He built the grandest structures, enjoyed the best the world offered, experienced all imaginable pleasure, and possessed all the power to do whatever he wanted.

But notice how Ecclesiastes starts and finishes the same way. It opens: *"Vanity of vanities, says the Preacher, vanity of vanities! All is vanity"* (Ecclesiastes 1:2). And closes with the same words: *"Vanity of vanities, says the Preacher; all is vanity"* (Ecclesiastes

12:8). He begins in emptiness and ends in emptiness. All the money in the world, and nothing changed.

Money might buy happiness, but the happiness wears off quickly. And when it does, you are left where you were without it. **Nothing bought with money can fill the void in the soul.** Nothing. After every purchase, given enough time, the emptiness returns. The grandest dream home loses its appeal and becomes ordinary in the eyes of its occupants. The brand-new device gets its first scratch and becomes just another object.

Some say it is about enjoying the journey rather than the destination. But at what cost? There is always a price to pay when you pursue something. The opportunity cost of making money is often the ability to enjoy money — and that is unfortunate. A lot of people who have put their life into building wealth do not know how to enjoy it.

The only worthy pursuit is the pursuit of God. Money can facilitate this if you learn about money from God. Biblical principles show how money can be used in the kingdom so that it adds to, rather than takes from, our enjoyment of God. Money is not dirty. It is a powerful tool that can be used as a way to exercise faith. Someone who has practised the biblical ways of money will likely grow in both holiness and wealth — simultaneously.

Most Christians subscribe to the idea of pursuing God, but many fall to the temptation of comparison. Comparing your financial situation with someone else's is a trap. You see the house, the car, the holiday. But what you won't see is what might be behind it — the sorrow, the anxiety, the fear, or the grip that the riches may be costing them. **Wealth without God always has a hidden cost.**

Proverbs 10:22 tells us how we know if wealth is from God: *"The blessing of the LORD makes rich, and he adds no sorrow with it."* That is the difference between accumulating money with God and without him — not the amount, not the appearance, but the sorrow. Or the absence of it. God-blessed wealth does not keep you up at night. It does not demand a tighter and tighter grip to hold together.

You cannot see another person's peace. Don't compare. Pursue God, not money — and guard your peace.

POWER TRIP

The more money you have, the more power you have. How you use that power is up to you. **God does not care about the amount of money a person has — he cares about how the person uses it.** In the parable of the talents, each servant was given a different amount to start with. The master's word to the faithful ones was not about how much they had been given, but what they did with it: *"Well done, good and faithful servant. You have been faithful over a little; I will set you over much"* (Matthew 25:21). The idea that every follower of Jesus should have roughly the same amount of money cannot be found in the Bible.

Not every believer should be poor, nor should every believer be rich. Having too little can make money have power over you. Having too much can also cause money to have power over you. Proverbs 30:8–9 captures this tension better than most: *"...give me neither poverty nor riches; feed me with the food that is needful for me, lest I be full and deny you and say, 'Who is the LORD?' or lest I be poor and steal and profane the name of my God."*

The issue is not the amount. The issue is whether money has power over you.

When money changes your view of God — either way — money is no longer serving you: you are serving money. If things go well financially and we praise God, we might just be praising the money. When things go badly and we don't involve God, we are letting money define our relationship with God. In either case, money becomes our teacher and our guide rather than the Holy Spirit. This is why every follower of Jesus needs to learn to have power over money, rather than letting money have power over them.

We must learn to conquer the power money can have on us. The church of Laodicea was very wealthy and thought they did not need God. Jesus' judgement was searingly blunt: *"For you say, I am rich, I have prospered, and I need nothing, not realising that you are wretched, pitiable, poor, blind, and naked"* (Revelation 3:17). **Their wealth was causing them to go lukewarm.** Yet Jesus does not leave them without hope. In Revelation 3:21 he says: *"The one who conquers, I will grant him to sit with me on my throne."* This is a remarkable invitation — but one that requires having control over money rather than being controlled by it.

We own the most expensive pug in the world — as far as I know. Just before she came into our lives, we had another pug that was run over at only twelve weeks old. We decided to get a second. While she was still a puppy, she had a fall and broke both front elbows. The whole family piled into the car and drove to the animal hospital. The news was not good. To fix her would cost the price of a small new car. The alternatives were amputation or putting her down.

Amputation was never going to happen — maybe if it were the back legs, because you can give them a wheelchair, but having no front legs doesn't work for dogs. As for putting her down, my children had just grieved the loss of their first dog a month earlier. The sound of their wailing was still too vivid, and I could not bear the thought of having them wail again, not this close to the last one.

I knew there was money sitting in our mortgage offset account. So I said to my wife: "We are going to use this money to take away the tears our children would otherwise shed." She agreed without hesitation. We made money work for us that day — it did exactly what it was supposed to do.

I knew then, more strongly than ever, what I had always believed: money is my servant.

THE HANDOVER

You can either live a life where money controls how you live, or live in a way where only God controls how you live. Letting go of money's grip takes both intention and time. It does not happen because you got baptised. The grip money has on us started in childhood — when we could not buy what we wanted, when we first desired something and realised we could not afford it. We all have a long history with money that needs to be redefined.

Money impacts almost every decision we make and, therefore impacts how we live out almost all of our faith. **Every money decision needs to be reframed as a faith decision.** Paul puts it plainly: *"But whoever has doubts is condemned if he eats, because the eating is not from faith. For whatever does not proceed from faith is sin"* (Romans 14:23). Paul is writing about food offered to idols, but the principle he lands on is universal — anything done outside of faith is sin. Money decisions are no exception.

You learn to make faith decisions through small financial decisions. Should you buy a coffee machine so you stop buying coffee from a café? Or is supporting your local café a way of building relationships with the owner and supporting a business that employs many staff? You need to ask God and make a faith-based decision — one led by your spiritual convictions, not a financial one.

Whether to rent or buy shouldn't be a purely financial decision but a matter of what God has given you the opportunity to pursue. Perhaps you should do neither — live at home, help with the rent, and support your parents while you can. But then again, some should just move out because their parents will not teach them independence while they are living at home. The matter of where and how you should live is not a finance decision; it is a faith-based one.

There are no black-and-white rules you can make with money because faith is never black-and-white. Faith works through the grey. **If faith were obvious, it would be called a fact.** Money decisions are not black-and-white. Money decisions are faith decisions, and like all faith decisions, you will need the help of the Holy Spirit.

Paul calls every believer to full surrender: *"I appeal to you therefore, brothers, by the mercies of God, to present your bodies as a living sacrifice, holy and acceptable to God, which is your spiritual worship"* (Romans 12:1). We have surrendered our lives to Jesus, and we hand over control to the Holy Spirit. This means we surrender the power to make money and the power to use it. We must submit both the accumulation and the expenditure to the Holy Spirit. He now tells us how to earn it and how to use it — which turns money matters into a matter of trust.

Money in the hands of a Christian is the currency of faith. We use money to exercise our trust in God. Money becomes a medium through which we build our relationship with him. We no longer make money-based decisions — we make God-based decisions with money. Money becomes a tool.

TWO EXTREMES

There are two errors Christians fall into when it comes to money, and they sit at opposite ends of the same spectrum. One is what might be called the poverty gospel. The other is the prosperity gospel. **Both distort the biblical picture and both need to be named clearly.**

The poverty gospel suggests that money is evil, that capitalism is demonic, and that owning nothing is godly. It sounds like the gospel because it borrows real truths. The writer of Hebrews describes the great saints of faith this way: *"These all died in faith, not having received the things promised, but having seen them and greeted them from afar, and having acknowledged that they were strangers and exiles on the earth"* (Hebrews 11:13).

This world is passing. We are citizens of another kingdom. We should live as foreigners. But the poverty gospel takes those truths too far. It makes people hate the world, while Jesus loved the world (John 3:16). It tries to live disconnected from the world, while God sends us into it (John 17:18). **The poverty gospel is not humility.**

The prosperity gospel is the complete opposite — and no less a distortion. It is not the gospel of the Lord Jesus Christ. It is a counterfeit, as a cubic zirconia is to a real diamond. It looks like the genuine thing from a distance, but it is not. The prosperity gospel loves the material world and lives in it as though there were no life after it. It teaches not only that God wants us wealthy, but that wealth and health are our entitlement as believers. **You could not distinguish someone living in the prosperity gospel from someone living entirely for this world — they look the same.**

God gives the power to create wealth. Deuteronomy 8:18 is clear: *"You shall remember the LORD your God, for it is he who gives you power to get wealth, that he may confirm his covenant that he swore to your fathers, as it is this day."* But he gives it so we can steward it for his kingdom, not consume it for ourselves.

The same is true for healing — James is direct: "*Is anyone among you sick? Let him call for the elders of the church, and let them pray over him, anointing him with oil in the name of the Lord; and the prayer of faith will save the one who is sick, and the Lord will raise him up*" (James 5:14–15). Healing is in his hands, not ours. So is wealth. **We are not entitled to anything.** Our job is stewardship.

We are called to steward whatever situation we are in. Even bad financial situations are not always the result of sin. In John 9, Jesus explicitly rejected the idea that suffering equals sin — "*neither this man nor his parents sinned*" (John 9:3). Excessive rain can drown a year's crops. Fire can destroy a year's inventory. People can be cheated, robbed, or born into poverty through no fault of their own. These are not punishments. They are consequences of living in a broken world — but they are also, in God's hands, opportunities for his glory to be displayed.

If you sense a preacher leaning towards either of these extremes, proceed with caution.

CHAPTER 2
FOLLOW THE MONEY

What you need to understand first about how money works.

ASSETS

Assets are things that hold value. They either lose value over time — depreciate — or become more valuable over time — appreciate. Cars and computers generally depreciate. Gold and houses generally appreciate.

Assets are priced by demand and supply. If there is a lot of something, it will be cheaper; if there is little of something, it will be worth more. **The greatest asset in the world is a human.** Each human is different, so the supply is one — and God's demand for them is enough to send his Son (John 3:16). Every human is priceless in God's kingdom.

The second greatest asset is the Earth. There is only one Earth, and we all need it to survive. The planet we inhabit is irreplaceable, and we need to learn to treat it with enormous love and respect. There is no other Earth — nothing that orbits a perfectly sized sun at the perfect radius so we don't get cooked and we don't freeze solid.

Within the Earth, there are things that are also valuable, but their value is mostly demand-driven. Old houses remain expensive because people want them; used cars become cheap because people don't. Their price — their value in money — is determined by what people want and how much of it exists.

PURCHASING POWER

The same money buys you less over time — in some sense, money depreciates. The five-dollar note in your pocket buys less than the five-dollar note in your pocket ten years ago — that is inflation at work. Inflation describes how you need more money to buy the same thing over time. When people say inflation is high, it usually means things cost more now than they did the same time last year.

One major reason money gets less valuable is the same reason any asset gets less valuable — an increase in supply. Money buys less over time because more money is created over time. In simplistic terms, money is created through central banks and through bank lending. Governments also increase the money supply, particularly when central banks purchase government debt. Let me explain.

HOW NEW MONEY IS PRINTED

The dollar used to be fixed to gold. In the US, ordinary people could exchange cash for gold at the bank until 1933. After that, only foreign governments could, but the dollar's value stayed tied to gold. This was known as the Gold Standard. In 1971, the US government ended the dollar's link to gold, turning it into a currency whose value depends on confidence rather than a fixed weight of metal. **The entire cash system is built on trust** — trust that the paper in your hand is worth something. If everyone stopped believing that, it would be worth nothing.

The reason the US government disconnected cash from gold was that the Gold Standard limited them from printing more money. When cash was connected to gold, creating more money generally required holding more gold or changing the value assigned to gold. They didn't want to do the former and could not meaningfully do the latter — so they simply "de-pegged" the dollar from the Gold Standard. This gave governments and central banks greater flexibility to fund public infrastructure, healthcare, social services, or war.

Governments borrow money by issuing IOUs called bonds, which are bought by investors such as banks, pension funds, and other governments. Central banks can also purchase government bonds, increasing the amount of money in the financial system. Banks also create new money whenever they make loans. There are other ways the money supply changes too, but they are beyond the scope of this book. **What matters is this: the money supply can increase over time**, and during COVID it increased rapidly in many countries.

Since the early 1970s, most countries have moved away from currencies backed by gold. Today, almost all major currencies are "floating," with their value determined largely by supply and demand in foreign exchange markets. This is why exchange rates rise and fall, making overseas holidays sometimes more expensive and sometimes cheaper.

Over time, as the money supply grows, the purchasing power of your money tends to decline — often without you doing anything.

MULTIPLICATION

Now you know: if you have money and do nothing, your money will depreciate like a car. Jesus told a story about a master and three servants. We met one of them in the last chapter. Here is how they started.

> "To one he gave five talents, to another two, to another one, to each according to his ability. Then he went away. He who had received the five talents went at once and traded with them, and he made five talents more. So also he who had the two talents made two talents more. But he who had received the one talent went and dug in the ground and hid his master's money."
> *(Matthew 25:15–18)*

You and I need to be like the other two — do something with it so that it multiplies.

Doing something involves risk. That's how God designed it. Consider a farmer. They spend money on seeds, fertiliser, and equipment to plow and plant — all of it pure risk because there is no guarantee of a harvest. But should the harvest be successful, the seed will multiply and be sold for multiples of the cost.

Doing something involves facing fear. The servant who buried his talent wasn't just unproductive — he was fearful. His exact explanation: *"I was afraid, and I went and hid your talent in the ground"* (Matthew 25:25). **Fear of taking a risk is a spiritual issue.** If money controls us through fear — fear of losing it, fear of investing wrongly, fear of not having enough — then money is still the master. Overcoming the fear of investing is an act of faith, not just financial maturity.

Holding onto money is not a wise strategy. Money should be made to work. Turning money into assets that grow is how we make money work for us like servants. Making money work is not a worldly thing — it is God's thing. We need to exercise authority over money and not have money exercise authority over us.

Converting money into assets shapes our character because it demands delayed gratification. You only have a finite amount of money at any given point in time — **if you invest, it simultaneously means you cannot spend.** This level of self-control is training for the soul. Most people will want to spend rather than invest, not because they don't believe in investing, but because they are obsessed with consuming. **Making money work by buying assets that appreciate is an active fight against consumerism.** Not spending is not enough — it's just the start. You need to then learn the joy of delayed gratification.

Like the joy of the farmer who reaps a harvest, there is joy in investing. God wired us to desire rewards — and there is real reward in seeing assets grow. We should seek to invest in both people, as God's greatest asset, and in investment assets that grow. It is not either / or. It is both.

Beware that investing can become its own kind of consuming. The portfolio replaces the shopping cart. Proverbs 23:4 says: *"Do not toil to acquire wealth; be discerning enough to desist."* God's kingdom has no place for burning yourself out to get rich. Neither the servant with five talents nor the servant with two had a target in mind. They took the risk, and it happened to double by the time they were held to account. **A target number is not the goal; the goal is being free from the love of money (1 Timothy 6:10).**

Passive investing doesn't need to be hard — simply investing in an index fund or a high-interest savings account is enough. Even in the parable, the master said: *"You ought to have invested my money with the bankers, and at my coming I should have received what was my own with interest..."* (Matthew 25:27).

And yes, investing sounds slow and is slow — that's the point. Multiplication doesn't just happen in the investment but in the individual. *"Wealth gained hastily will dwindle, but whoever gathers little by little will increase it"* (Proverbs 13:11). **There is no race. Don't compete — there is no competition.** Don't turn something good into greed or pride. We aren't called to be asset managers; we are just stewards learning the biblical principles of money to make us more like Christ.

COMPOUNDING

When you hear about investing, you will hear about the term 'compounding.' This phenomenon is not exclusively financial; it can be found in the way God created the world. When bacteria multiply, one bacterium can turn into 512 cells within three hours, but after just nine more hours, it will have multiplied to 68,719,476,736 cells. This kind of growth can also be found in investing.

In financial terms, compound growth is simply this: your money makes money, and then the money it earns makes even more money, along with your original investment. The growth is compounding. **A single dollar invested at a modest return does not just grow — it compounds like a snowball rolling down a mountain.**

This is why investing as early as you can is sound advice. Parents who invest their children's money get the compounding effect starting early. On the flip side, every year you delay is not just a year lost; it is a year of lost compounding. **You do not have to be wealthy to begin. You just have to begin.**

This is also why debt is so dangerous. **Compounding works both ways.** The same force that grows your investments is the force that grows your debt when you carry a balance. Credit card interest compounds against you with the same relentless power that investment returns compound for you. Understanding this is not just financial literacy — it is freedom.

FIGHTING INFLATION

Storing money in a transaction account is not enough. Investing seems daunting, but it does not start with opening a brokerage account. It starts with learning to do research. You can simply start by learning how to invest in a high-interest savings account (HISA). These usually have promotional interest rates for the first few months — moving your money from one HISA to another is a great way to take advantage of promotional rates. Applications for a HISA do not affect your credit rating or score because it is your money, not borrowed money, so you can switch around as much as you want.

Later, you may look into investing in broad-based index funds or ETFs — listed on the public stock exchange. The easiest way to think of an index fund is like buying into a whole industry or the best of the top companies, rather than just one. The firm offering the index fund or ETF allocates your investment across the right collection of companies and regularly adjusts for the best outcome. Index funds can also generate income through dividends, making them popular with retirees. You will need to research what the best brokerage is to get started — many companies have made this process very simple.

After index funds and ETFs, you may consider becoming an active investor. Those with HISAs or ETFs are called passive investors — not a bad title. It simply means they make a purchase and move on without actively managing their investment.

Active investors actively manage their investments — businesses, properties, share trading, crypto, derivatives, and other financial products. Investment properties sit in this category because purchasing and managing a property and its tenants is complex and time-consuming.

Learning to be an active investor is a skill — it requires the same discipline as any other skill. You need education, mentors, and an active learning community. Without these things, success is possible but difficult to achieve and difficult to sustain. Those wanting to invest in a business need business mentors. Those looking to trade stocks need to learn how to read charts and understand industries and markets. Those moving capital into crypto need a clear entry and exit process. Those purchasing an investment property need to understand exactly what kind of property they want and what yields it will produce. **You cannot become an active investor overnight, nor by yourself.**

I know what it feels like to think you understand something you don't. I started investing in crypto before I read a single book on investing — and I paid for that arrogance. The mistakes I made were there in plain sight in the books. It was truly humbling. **Whatever category of investing you pursue, invest in your own education first.** The enthusiasm and confidence you feel at the start are not the same as preparation.

Active investment is not to be done alone. *"Where there is no guidance, a people falls, but in an abundance of counselors there is safety"* (Proverbs 11:14). *"Without counsel plans fail, but with many advisers they succeed"* (Proverbs 15:22). **It is better to make a little with the counsel of others than to think you know better and lose it all.** A little gained is better than a big loss.

We all want to think we are the smartest — that we know something others do not. In time, you will realise there are a lot more people smarter than you. *"Do you see a man who is wise in his own eyes? There is more hope for a fool than for him"* (Proverbs 26:12). Don't be that person. Ask me how I know.

CHAPTER 3
THE TITHE

This is the chapter you will wish I didn't write.

If I didn't have something to offer, I wouldn't have written it. At the very least, it will remind you why you already do it. At best, it will show you why the tithe is a spiritual weapon — not a religious act of duty.

Before I explain, let me tell you what it has done for me. I have never had a spiritual recession. I have never seriously doubted my faith. I believe tithing is a significant reason why — it has kept my relationship with God alive in a way nothing else has. I have tithed consistently for over twenty years, and I am convinced that consistency is what has helped build my faith. Every time I tithe, my faith grows. It ties my finances to my faith, and like any investment, it compounds over time.

ABRAHAM AND MELCHIZEDEK

The idea that tithing is merely an Old Testament obligation — something from the law of Moses, now superseded by grace — misses the origin entirely. **The tithe did not begin with Moses.** It began with Abraham.

Genesis 14:18–20 records a mysterious encounter that Abram had (later in Genesis 17 God gives him a new name: Abraham). Abram had just rescued his nephew Lot in a military engagement and returned with significant plunder. Then, out of nowhere, Melchizedek — King of Salem, priest of God Most High — arrives with bread and wine. He blesses Abram. And in receiving that blessing, Abram gives a tenth of everything to this mysterious priest.

This is the first tithe in scripture. It predates the law by several centuries. And it matters enormously, because Abraham is not responding to a legal obligation. He is responding to an encounter with God — mediated through a priest whose origin is unexplained, whose genealogy is unrecorded, and who appears in the text almost as a divine figure.

The writer of Hebrews takes this up in chapter 7. Melchizedek, he explains, is *"without father or mother or genealogy, having neither beginning of days nor end of life, but resembling the Son of God"* (Hebrews 7:3). We cannot know if Melchizedek was Jesus himself before he came into the world — pre-incarnate — or simply a representation of Jesus in the Old Testament. What is important is that Melchizedek points us toward Jesus, our great High Priest: *"Since then we have a great high priest who has passed through the heavens, Jesus, the Son of God, let us hold fast our confession"* (Hebrews 4:14).

The writer of Hebrews draws the thread forward. When we bring our tithe to the church, we are not merely giving to an institution — we are giving to God. We are doing what the tribes of Israel did when they gave to the Levites. Israel wasn't tithing to the Levites; they were tithing to God. The earthly recipient might be the offering box or a church bank account, but the true recipient is the Risen King. We do not tithe because the law says so. **We tithe because Abraham — the father of faith —**

modelled it as an act of faith. We give because it is what people of faith do.

God does not want our tithe as much as he wants a people who tithe. Tithing sets us free from the love of money. If it were not a big deal, everyone would be doing it — and it would have no power. But because it requires real faith, it produces something real.

The order matters. When Abraham gave his tenth, he gave it after Melchizedek blessed him — not before, and not in order to receive something. **The tithe was a response to God's goodness, not a lever to pull on it.** This is the heart of tithing that is so easily lost. The tithe is not a financial transaction — it is a relational one.

In Malachi, God commands: *"Bring the full tithe into the store-house... and thereby put me to the test... if I will not open the windows of heaven for you and pour down for you a blessing until there is no more need"* (Malachi 3:10). **This invitation comes from a place of grief, not barter.** The hearts of the Israelites had grown hard and distant. God was not setting up a reward scheme. Through Malachi, God was pleading with a people he loved, saying: just try it so I can show you who I am. He invited them to test him because that was what their hardness required. He wanted to give to them — he was looking for a way to their heart.

For us, God should not need to take this posture. We are not a people whose hearts are far from God — or at least, we should not be. We tithe not to test God, not to trigger a blessing, not to prove a principle. **We tithe because we love him.** Because he has already blessed us. Because Abraham showed us that the right response to an encounter with God is an open hand representing our open heart. God should not have to plead with us the way he pleaded with Israel. We already know the kind of God he is.

But should you need to test him, the offer still stands.

WHY JESUS DIDN'T TEACH TITHING

If I write an autobiography, I will never mention that I take my shoes off before I enter my home. It's so obvious I won't mention it. Nor will you ever hear me teach my children why I believe it is good to take your shoes off before entering the house. This is the exact same reason why you will not hear Jesus teach about the tithe.

Jesus didn't teach tithing because he didn't need to. Jesus was raised as a Jew, and his mission was to Jews (Matthew 15:24). Every observant Jew gave the tithe, just like every Korean — the heritage of this writer — takes their shoes off before they enter the house. Expecting Jesus to teach his disciples about tithing is like expecting to hear me teach my children about taking their shoes off before they come in; it was a given. When Jesus does mention tithing, it is not to teach it — it is to rebuke the Pharisees:

> *"Woe to you, scribes and Pharisees, hypocrites! For you tithe mint and dill and cumin, and have neglected the weightier matters of the law: justice and mercy and faithfulness. These you ought to have done, without neglecting the others." (Matthew 23:23)*

Notice what Jesus does not say. He does not say stop tithing. He assumes it — and rebukes them for using it as a substitute for the things that matter most. That's why there is no teaching on tithing in the Gospels. It didn't need teaching.

Jewish people tithed because it was written into the Law of Moses. This is not the origin of tithing but its national application. The principle came first. God designed the tithe as an instrument — a way of life to keep his people close to him. The tithe was a reflection of the importance of the Levites, who prepared all things related to the worship of God. The tithes of all the other tribes went to one tribe — the Levites — so that this tribe would dedicate themselves to the nation's connection with God. God made this provision explicit:

> *"And the LORD said to Aaron, 'You shall have no inheritance in their land, neither shall you have any portion among them. I am your portion and your inheritance among the people of Israel. ... To the Levites I have given every tithe in Israel for an inheritance, in return for their service that they do, their service in the tent of meeting.'" (Numbers 18:20–21)*

Jesus lived as a Jew and gave like a Jew. Tithing was part of his life — and so, naturally, it should be part of ours.

FIRST FRUITS

Tithing should be your first financial goal. I'm not aiming to introduce a new law but rather provide clarity, especially for someone starting out.

Proverbs 3:9 says to honour the LORD with the firstfruits of all your produce. I take that literally: God gets the first portion. Before the government, before anything else. So I tithe on gross income — 10% of everything my employer pays me, before tax. For businesses, this means 10% of gross profit.

In practice this takes some working out because employers withhold PAYG before your pay ever reaches your account. Some people land on tithing after tax, on what actually arrives in the bank. I understand that, and I am not going to argue with anyone about it. What matters far more than the calculation is that the first portion goes to God.

Keep it simple.

Tithing doesn't need to be the ceiling of your giving. After you tithe, consider putting aside an extra 1% for other charitable giving, then try 2% and increase it each year. A great goal after giving the tithe would be the double tithe. The tithe goes to the church, and the second portion to charitable giving or missions work. Once you find the joy of giving, keep going bigger.

We have pushed into percentages that frightened us. We asked ourselves, would this put our family into debt? Would our children resent us for giving to others at their expense? So far, we have not gone into debt, and our children have never been deprived of clothes, meals, or experiences. In fact, as we pushed into new levels of giving, we have found ourselves experiencing even greater levels of freedom and enjoyment.

PRACTICAL APPLICATION

Can I start lower?

Yes — starting somewhere is better than not starting. Any start is a tremendous act of faith. Remember that fear is normal. Fear is a sign that genuine faith is required. So if giving even a lower percentage feels scary, it means you are exercising faith. If you are starting at a smaller percentage, don't be surprised if you quickly end up at 10%.

Do I calculate everything?

Pocket money? Monetary gifts? Centrelink payments?

Tithe on income. Wages, gifts, Centrelink — count them. For anything that runs like a business, including a rental property, tithe on the profit, not the takings. Rent absorbed by loan interest was never income in the first place.

Tithing government payments is a great idea if that is your primary source of income; the amount is small but the faith required is disproportionately large. Don't tithe so you can pass an audit. Tithe so you can grow in faith.

Jesus pointed to the widow who gave two copper coins — the smallest amount given that day, yet counted as more than all the others:

> *"And he sat down opposite the treasury and watched the people putting money into the offering box. Many rich people put in large sums. And a poor widow came and put in two small copper coins, which make a penny. And he called his disciples to him and said to them, 'Truly, I say to you, this widow has put in more than all those who are contributing to the offering box. For they all contributed out of their abundance, but she out of her poverty has put in everything she had, all she had to live on.'" (Mark 12:41–44)*

What is given must be given freely and without compulsion: *"Each one must give as he has decided in his heart, not reluctantly or under compulsion, for God loves a cheerful giver"* (2 Corinthians 9:7). If tithing makes you smile because of the faith and love you are exercising towards God, you are doing what only the few will do.

Can I give things other than money?

Not as a substitute for money. Some say they give their time, expertise, and energy to the church as part of their tithe. This is shrewdness gone wrong. The tithe was designed to loosen your grip on money — substituting time for money is the complete opposite. Calculating your time and efforts, however valuable the market says they are, does not give you the right to force the church to receive your services in lieu of your tithe. Instead of receiving your tithe, the church is getting your time without its consent. That is just strange.

If you have an issue with giving the full tithe, own it. Admit it and ask God for faith to work through it — the grip of money is real, and tithing is one of God's tools to break it.

Can I spend money on church instead of giving to the church? Can I give to other organisations as my tithe?

Tithing is about surrendering control of 10% — which means the decision of where it goes must also be surrendered. When you spend money on things the church needs, you are making the decision — that is not surrender; that is management. When the tribes of Israel gave to the Levites, they had no authority to direct or restrict how those tithes were used. If you want to make financial decisions for the church, make them from your own money, not God's.

In my view, the tithe is the way to sow into your church — and I hold that with conviction. But I also recognise that giving is complicated for many people. Some are between churches. Some carry wounds from church that make giving feel impossible. Some are already generous givers — to missions, to charities, to causes that reflect the heart of God — and are working their way toward a church they can call home. If that is you, I am not here to dismiss what you are already doing.

What I would say is this: aim to move your tithe toward your church. Let it become your primary recipient. The structure of the tithe is part of what makes it formative — not just for you, but for the family of faith you belong to. You surrender to a community whose leaders answer to God for how it is used, and whose members share the work of stewarding it well.

Remember, the principle of tithing is learning to let go of control.

PART TWO
WORK

CHAPTER 4
THE ART OF WORK

NEVER WORK FOR MONEY

If you work only for money, money will determine your work. Once you decide what you will do and how hard you will work based on your pay, you have set the ceiling on your own value. If you think a $25-an-hour worker should only do certain things, you will stay at $25 an hour if that's all you do. But if you work as though you are worth $40 an hour, take on opportunities beyond what others at your level would take, and succeed in them, the current employer may not pay you $40 but your next employer probably will.

People hand over money when they find something of value. Employers pay when they believe the value you bring will exceed what they give up in money. Clients pay when they believe your company brings value that others can't. **This is why we need to work as though we are working for the next job we want, not the present job we have.** Work future-present, not past-present. Past-present is: this is all I know, so this is all I will give. Future-present is: this is what I want to do well in the future, so I will take the steps to develop it now. A future-present mindset will naturally attract more pay — because you are chasing value, not chasing money.

Consider how most successful artists, entrepreneurs, and athletes started out working for free, or close to it. They put in the work while there was no pay. The money came after they produced something of value. If they had only worked towards their present value, they would have stayed as amateurs, not professionals. Most famous musicians worked hard while earning virtually nothing, before anyone knew them. That pattern is consistent across most successful people: virtually unknown, almost always underpaid — until the world discovered the value of what they had built for most of their lives.

Once you work for money, money will own you. You will move from job to job looking for higher pay rather than looking to increase the value of your work. The goal as an employee is to move towards work that pays you for your contribution and your expertise, not for your time.

The best jobs reward outcomes and skill rather than hours. This principle holds true for businesses: money is attracted to value, not volume. If anyone can be trained to do your job within six months, you are being paid for time, not expertise. If anyone can replace what your company can offer in one year, you are not creating value. Valuable skills and valuable products take a long time to develop. This is why even a fast-food manager is paid disproportionately more than the person at the register — expertise and experience, not hours. This is why a tech company with genuine expertise commands high margins while dozens of competitors fight over cents.

YOU ARE NOT YOUR WORK

When we watch the Olympics, we are inspired by people who have dedicated their lives to one thing. When we eat at a fine dining restaurant, we are in awe of the chef who has given themselves entirely to their craft. People who have dedicated themselves to the perfection of one thing are indeed admirable — but whether we want to be admired like this is a very important question. Rather than asking "What do I want to dedicate my life to?" I think it is more important to ask, **"How do I want to be remembered, and by whom?"**

When you die, at your funeral, people will not talk about what you achieved. They will talk about how you made them feel — how you affected them personally. **If your ambition in life is to achieve many things, be aware that in the end, very few of those achievements will be mentioned.** When I conducted my uncle's funeral, we didn't talk once about what he did for work. We talked about what he meant to us, what he did for us. I shared memories of how he always let me stay at his place and how generous he was to my mum and us.

The value of work is not in the work itself, but in how you go about it. Your work is not more valuable to the kingdom because you are a pastor, a doctor, or a teacher. It is more valuable when you go about it as though you are working for the Lord. Paul told the Colossian bondservants — and by extension anyone working under another's authority — "Whatever you do, work heartily, as for the Lord and not for men" (Colossians 3:23). What you do is not as important as how you do it.

It is dangerous to tie our worth to the value we provide others. **Our worth does not come from our work.** It comes from being God's sons and daughters (Romans 8:14; Galatians 4:6–7). When we make work give us worth, we seek the kind of work that makes us feel good about ourselves. If we pursue that type of work too hard, work becomes a false idol — something we devote ourselves to because it makes us feel good. We end up worshipping work.

You are not your work. What you do is not the measure of your life.

SERVE FIRST

Jesus said that he came not to be served but to serve: *"For even the Son of Man came not to be served but to serve, and to give his life as a ransom for many"* (Mark 10:45). That is the model. The better question to ask young people is not "What do you want to do when you grow up?" but "Who do you want to serve, and how do you want to serve them?" Service connects passion to people. "Follow your passion" is half-baked advice. **The full advice is: follow the passion that will serve the people you want to serve.**

Some of the most dedicated workers are those with a personal reason to serve. If your child suffers from a particular illness, you will be passionate about seeing other children with that illness supported. **Passion needs to be anchored in people, not just in interests.**

Young people need to be taught to serve. This is why working in retail or hospitality at a young age matters — they learn the art of good service, even if it is just doing their allocated task well so the team can function. Learning how to be a good employee is not a waste — if you have learnt how you want to be managed, you can manage others well.

In my first job at 14, I worked from 4 p.m. to midnight on Wednesdays as a dough maker and kitchen hand in a pizza shop. From 4 p.m. there would be two of us out back — from 9 p.m. it would be just me. One particular Wednesday I was exhausted and couldn't bear the thought of working until midnight, so I asked the other person if they could take my shift. When they said yes, I went to the manager and told him the other person was going to close and I was going home at 9 p.m. He told me it was not for me to decide such things — and told me not to come back.

It was a brutal lesson on what it meant to be a good employee: let managers make manager decisions. Since then, I ask my manager before I take leave — I give them information for them to make decisions. I've learnt how to be an employee and, in turn, it has taught me how to be a good manager.

If you focus on serving, you can start working immediately. *"Whatever your hand finds to do, do it with your might."* (Ecclesiastes 9:10) If you focus on finding your passion, it may be a long time before you are serving anyone. Even from the age of twelve, Jesus knew where he belonged (Luke 2:42). When his parents found him in the temple after three days of searching, his response was untroubled: *"Why were you looking for me? Did you not know that I must be in my Father's house?"* (Luke 2:49) Yet he spent the next eighteen years in the family trade (Luke 3:23).

Luke tells us nothing about the carpentry. What he tells us is what was happening to Jesus: he *"increased in wisdom and in stature and in favor with God and man"* (Luke 2:52). That is the fruit of good labour. He did not wait for the most strategically meaningful role. He did what was in front of him.

Work begets work. When you are actively working, other opportunities open. You meet the right people. Your world gets bigger. You cannot find your purpose locked alone at home. You are called to serve others — so you need to understand them and you cannot understand them without being with them.

This is why you don't need to chase promotion. If you are doing it God's way, God will promote you. *"The heart of man plans his way, but the LORD establishes his steps"* (Proverbs 16:9). By all means, plan. Set direction. But let God give you each step — you don't need to define or demand them. I watched a dear friend go from entry-level quality officer to executive general manager without ever striving for it. He simply served well at every level.

Don't climb the corporate ladder. Hold on to God and let him pull you up.

HARD TO REPLACE

The best kind of work is work where you are hard to replace. *"Do you see a man skillful in his work? He will stand before kings; he will not stand before obscure men"* (Proverbs 22:29). There are several ways to achieve this — you only need one or two to become genuinely indispensable.

Relationships. Consider the partners of a professional services firm. They share in the profit because they hold the client relationships. If they leave, the clients leave with them. When the cost of losing a partner exceeds the cost of keeping them, the organisation will keep them — even if they do not particularly like them.

Expertise. Some people know exactly how certain things work. Their knowledge is rare or expensive to find elsewhere. It is cheaper to keep them around even when their expertise is not constantly needed — because losing them would cost a lot more when things go wrong or things change. Even with the entire internet available, there are still things that are not documented anywhere. You want to be the person people turn to for those things.

Specialised experience. Many people have experience, but when you have specific experience that others do not, you become difficult to replace. In medicine, some specialists further specialise in a specific procedure — every surgeon in that field might know what the surgery involves, but patients with particular conditions are referred to them specifically because no one else has done it as many times.

Creativity. Trust in creative work is hard to build and very sticky once established. The process of a business working with an individual to develop a brief and create even a concept is gruelling. But when it works, it is magical — and the bond formed through that shared struggle is difficult to break. When companies find a marketing agency or graphic designer they trust, they stay with them. The cost of switching feels too high.

Leadership. The world will always need more leaders because there will always be more people who need leading — and people are difficult to lead. The best leaders know how to lead other leaders. The top leaders of organisations are paid not for what they do, but for who they lead. It takes a unique person to bring the best out of other leaders.

ALL WORK IS WORK

If you only value paid work, your life will be miserable. You will not work hard on your relationships, your health, your church, or the things that actually enrich your life. You must value all work as work, whether income is attached to it or not.

If your mother only valued paid work, she would not have loved you the way she did. If you value paid work above unpaid work, you will not love your children as you should. Unpaid work is not less important. Prioritising paid work can mean the people who matter most to you only get whatever is left over after work is done — if there is much left. One day that person might just have a well-paying job with no one to enjoy the earnings with.

Lose the concept of paid and unpaid work altogether. All work is working for God. Whether the work results in pay or not, we work because we sense it is the work God has given us to do — *"for we are his workmanship, created in Christ Jesus for good works,* *which God prepared beforehand, that we should walk in them"* (Ephesians 2:10). And when we work for God like this, we can trust that God will provide — through whatever means — for all the kinds of work we do. The employer becomes the channel, not the source.

When you start to see money as God providing for you rather than as an exchange for your services, it changes both how you look at money and how you look at work. You will not let your pay determine your effort. You will give your best regardless of pay — and might find yourself promoted without having aimed for it. You will do volunteer and unpaid work in a different way because you will see money not as compensation for your work, but as God's goodness in his provision.

God is the source of income, the security you seek, and the only one who can give you true stability. *"And my God will supply every need of yours according to his riches in glory in Christ Jesus"* (Philippians 4:19).

WORKING FOR GOD

In the parable of the prodigal son, both brothers had the wrong attitude toward work. The younger son did not understand why he had to work — he just wanted to spend. The older son worked hard but worked for money. His reaction to his brother's return reveals everything:

> "But he was angry and refused to go in. His father came out and entreated him, but he answered his father, 'Look, these many years I have been serving you, and I never disobeyed your command, yet you never gave me a young goat, that I might celebrate with my friends. But when this son of yours came, *who has devoured*

> *your property with prostitutes, you killed the fattened calf for him!'"* (Luke 15:28–30)

He was furious. He was obsessed with money, not realising there was always more than enough.

Both brothers were miserable. Only the father demonstrates what actually matters — not work, not money, but relationships. Paul puts it plainly: *"You did not receive the spirit of slavery to fall back into fear, but you have received the Spirit of adoption as sons, by whom we cry, 'Abba! Father!'"* (Romans 8:15). The older son worked like a slave. The younger son was enslaved to money. Neither is the model. **We are to work like sons** — because the work the Father gives is both good for us and will bring the best out of us so that we can bring good into the world.

Working for God does not mean working for a church or a missions organisation. It does not mean your boss is a Christian or your output saves lives. **It means one thing: working as though God gave you the work to do.** If you are studying, study as though God wrote the course. If you are working in a café, serve the customer as though the café owner is God himself.

Who you work for is more important than the work you do. If you work for your salary, that is your master. If you work for your manager, they become your master. But if you work for God, an entirely different experience becomes available.

Remember who you work for. We work for God; he is our manager, master, and boss. Our work is not limited to paid work, church work, or missions work; rather, it is everything he gives us to do — because we trust that the work he gives us is not only suited for us but also brings out the best in us.

CHAPTER 5
WORK IN THE REAL WORLD

PREPARE THE FIELD

Everyone wants the house first. The house comes last.

> *"Prepare your work outside, get everything ready for yourself in the field and after that build your house." (Proverbs 24:27)*

The focus must be on building skills to earn. Get your finances in order before your furnishings. Get your earning going before your living. Without earning, there is no tithing, saving, investing, giving or even spending. Earning comes before everything else. And if you do not have a field to prepare, you must be the field. Prepare yourself.

You are the most important asset you will ever own. Invest accordingly.

Too many people walk away from school having decided they are not learners. This is not true. They just haven't found what they are drawn to yet. School, at its best, does two things. It teaches you how to learn. And it reveals what you are naturally drawn to. The real discovery is not the certificate. It is the curiosity. You can take that with you and multiply it for the rest of your life. **Formal education is optional. Learning is not.**

One of the fastest ways to learn is to read. But you have to fall in love with reading first.

Reading was once a privilege. For most of human history, access to books was restricted to the wealthy and the powerful. Ordinary people did not get to learn from the accumulated wisdom of others. Today, every library, every bookshop, every phone screen gives you access to knowledge that previous generations could only dream of. But because reading is now compulsory in school, we have taken one of the most extraordinary gifts in human history and turned it into homework. And everyone loathes homework. That was the case for me.

I only found the joy of reading at nineteen. I picked up the thickest novel I could find and discovered I wasn't a reluctant reader. I had just never found the right book. Every book prescribed to me in high school was Shakespeare or fantasy — both genres I didn't enjoy. If you don't love reading, you just haven't found the right author yet.

It is not homework. It is a superpower.

Reading is how you learn from other people's mistakes without paying for them yourself. It is accelerated growth. Decades of someone's hard-won experience distilled into pages you can absorb in a week. There is no faster shortcut to wisdom. Podcasts are good; books are better. There is only so much you can say in a podcast. The depth is in the pages.

When I choose a book, I scan the contents. I pick a chapter I think I might enjoy. I read it. If I find myself wanting more, I buy it. If I'm grinding through it — no matter how many people say it's essential — I put it down. Reading is more important than any single book. Guard the joy of it. I have made peace with the fact that I will not read every good book. I am okay with this because there are still plenty I will enjoy that I have yet to read.

If you want to invest in your children, don't just pay for tutoring. Incentivise them to read. Help them find the book that makes them fall in love with books. That one discovery will compound for the rest of their lives.

Preparing the field is not a one-time event. It is a lifelong habit. And sometimes that means learning things you never expected to learn.

I never learnt to dance. I had no interest in it. Then, at forty, one of my closest friends asked me to be his groomsman. Part of the role was a surprise groomsman dance. All the other groomsmen were years younger than me. The song was fast — Nayeon's POP. It was hard. I practised each move in front of a mirror for hours over many weeks. On the day, I kept up. I didn't bring shame to the family.

I've only performed that routine once. I still can't dance. But here is what I didn't expect — doing it made me confident in ways I can't fully put into words. I don't use that skill. I may never use it again. But the act of learning something hard, something outside my comfort zone, changed something in me. After that, I felt like I could do anything.

That is the real return on investment. It is not always the skill itself. It is the confidence that comes from proving to yourself that you can still learn. That confidence will accelerate everything else you do.

The field is you. The more you build yourself, the greater the value you can bring. Good employers notice, and they invest in people who invest in themselves. The same is true in business — clients can tell when a company is reinvesting rather than just taking profit. Growth attracts growth.

WORKING IN THE MARKETPLACE

There is no such thing as secular and spiritual work. There is no Christian and non-Christian vocation. When Jesus worked as a carpenter for most of his life, was he doing secular work? Was he not the Son of God during that time?

Working for God means working to serve the world he created. God created trade — the exchange of goods and services and the organisations that make it possible. It was there in the first command: fill the earth, subdue it, have dominion over it (Genesis 1:28). Business is a good thing because it is a God thing — a way human beings help each other.

A business does not need to be a "Christian business" to be blessed by God. There are, of course, businesses that do not help people — businesses you should be cautious about working in, because it is difficult to serve a company that is not serving the world. The businesses that grow wheat so we can eat bread may not be transforming the world in visible ways — but they are surely serving it. **That is enough.**

Some see being an employee as inferior to owning a business. It isn't. Whether you build a business or work in one, choose what will grow you most. For young people and those starting out, there is real value in a season of fixed employment. Those fixed hours become the backbone your week is built around. That structure builds discipline, and discipline is what makes you consistent. Consistency is where growth comes from.

PRINCIPLES FOR YOUR 20S, 30S, AND BEYOND

The habits you form early compound just as your investments do. Many people spend their 40s and 50s trying to undo what they normalised in their 30s — debt they never paid off, giving they never started, a savings rhythm they never built. The cost of starting late is real. These are not optional extras for the especially disciplined Christian. They are the ordinary habits of anyone who wants to hold money lightly for the rest of their life.

Wherever you are starting from, here is the order I would suggest: earning with tithing, then saving, then investing. Establish the tithe early. Leave it, and it only gets harder. If you don't save before you invest, you risk debt when the unexpected arrives. Follow the order.

Stage 1 — Build the Foundation

Most people do this in their 20s and 30s. If you are starting later, start here regardless.

Live Light

Keep debt to a minimum — or better yet, don't have debt at all. Watch out for credit cards, especially without a stable income. Never use Buy Now, Pay Later products (like Afterpay). Tithe as often as you get paid — learn to give while your earnings are small so that later, when you earn more, it will feel natural. Set regular savings targets, something that stretches you, and hit them. The feeling of hitting a goal you did not think you could reach is worth chasing. Keep your costs down. If you are tithing and saving diligently, you are probably already doing this. Do not buy things you cannot afford, and do not use an expensive purchase as motivation to work harder. If you really want something, work harder first and pay for it in full.

Get to Work

Get a job that will challenge you. Never stop looking for new challenges. If you cannot find them where you are, go somewhere you can. New skills build confidence.

Resist Temptation

Do not take out a car loan; paying interest on a depreciating asset is a double loss. Drive a car you can afford and use the money you would have wasted on a car loan to save or invest. Buy what you need with money you have saved, not with debt. Do not project a future pay rise into a present purchase — that is how you end up changing jobs for money rather than for growth. If you end up in debt, you may end your career before it has even started — settling for a job you don't want because of money you desperately need.

Be Independent

If you are living at home, start paying rent or contributing to household expenses — but if your parents prefer you to save for a house, honour them and do so. If you are renting and living independently, then well done.

Shout Others

You have been frugal — now learn to enjoy your resources with others. Spending on others doubles the fruit: you feel good giving, and you invest in a relationship. Once you have a good rhythm, consider a missions fund — a separate account with a small regular contribution. Use it to go on missions yourself, bless others, or give to needs as you see them.

Stage 2 — Build Wealth

Once the foundation is in place, build on it.

Build an Investment Strategy

Consider buying a home or starting to invest — ideally both over time. In Australia, houses have generally outperformed apartments over the long term, though this varies by location and market conditions. This is why if you buy an apartment, aim to pay it off as fast as possible so you can release equity faster (equity is the portion of the property you own outright). If you buy a house, avoid interest-only loans (these are tools for investors leveraging existing equity, not for building your first property), pay down the principal, and use an offset account to minimise interest and accelerate the loan.

Not everyone should buy property. If you are not yet ready, or if the numbers don't stack up in your market, put money into a low-cost index fund — a diversified ETF through the ASX is a straightforward starting point — and let compounding do its work. Superannuation is also doing this quietly in the background. Don't ignore it.

The goal is not to own property. The goal is to build assets that grow while you sleep.

Stage 3 — Build Legacy

This is the season of distribution. In the earlier stages, you build; now the question becomes: what for?

Don't break the habits you built getting here. The disciplines that carried you this far are the same ones that will carry you through. The temptation in this season is to relax — to feel like the hard work is done. It isn't. It just looks different.

Focus on Your Health

This is also the season to take your health seriously if you have not already. The decisions you make about your body in your 40s and 50s will determine the quality of your life in your elderly years. Invest in your health as an act of stewardship. As they say, the best time to plant a tree was twenty years ago — the next best time is now.

Help Others Climb Their Mountains

Shift your focus to the growth of others — your children, your mentees, your peers. Spend money on memories. Experiences with people you love accumulate value in a way that possessions do not. Use your time and money to build and solidify your network. Continue to serve others and add value wherever you are placed.

Enjoy It

The ability to enjoy what you have worked for is itself a gift from God — *"Everyone also to whom God has given wealth and possessions and power to enjoy them... this is the gift of God"* (Ecclesiastes 5:19). Enjoyment in this season is not self-indulgence — it is receiving God's gift with open hands. The person who cannot enjoy what God has given is not more holy.

Partner and Sponsor

This is also the season for legacy giving — not one-off generosity but consistent, sustained investment in causes, churches, and people you want to bless over years. Begin thinking now about where your wealth will go when you are gone, and start directing some of it while you are still alive to see the fruit.

Plan Your Death

Get a will. This is not morbid — it is stewardship. If you do not decide where your wealth goes, someone else will decide for you, and it may not reflect your values, your faith, or the people and causes you care about. A will is one of the most concrete expressions of what you actually believe about money. It is your last act of generosity. Do not leave it until it is too late to do it well.

Do not stop growing. Stay generous. Stay in the game — you don't know when you will be called home.

CHAPTER 6
THE SABBATH

NO WEEKENDS OFF

For most of history, there was no such thing as a weekend.

The two-day weekend we enjoy today has its roots in the Sabbath convictions of Jewish and Christian communities. Jewish businesses closed on Saturday because the Sabbath runs from sunset on Friday to sunset on Saturday. Christians gathered on Sunday in celebration of the resurrection. Over time, workplaces recognised both, and labour reforms in many countries made it permanent.

Take away those convictions, and your days off would be rostered by whoever owns the business.

Throughout most of history, ordinary people worked whenever work needed to be done. There were kings and nobles, merchants and priests and soldiers. But the overwhelming majority were farmers and labourers. Statistically, you and I would have been among them.

They rested when they were sick, when a religious festival stopped the work, or when there was simply no work to do.

Farming has its seasons — sowing and harvest, dawn until dusk for weeks at a time, then quiet. But finishing on Friday and knowing two days were yours? Unimaginable.

Don't take weekends for granted. Many people in the world don't enjoy the privilege.

CREATED FOR MORE THAN WORK

Your Sabbath matters more than you think. Sabbath isn't just a command — it's embedded within creation. God commanded it because it was essential, not optional. We don't observe the Sabbath so we can be the most productive workers in the next six days; we don't rest so we can work hard. **We are called to rest so we can remember who we are.** Forget who you are, and work will start to master you.

When Adam was created, he woke up sometime on the sixth day (Genesis 1:26–27). His first full day of being a human was on the seventh day of creation — the day God rested:

> *"And on the seventh day God finished his work that he had done, and he rested on the seventh day from all his work that he had done. So God blessed the seventh day and made it holy, because on it God rested from all his work that he had done in creation" (Genesis 2:2–3).*

Adam entered the world into Sabbath. The order is incredibly important. Adam was created first for rest, for enjoyment, for pleasure, for fun. He did not enter the world to start working. He was not God's servant; he was created in God's image and likeness to share in his joy.

We were not made to be God's labourers. We were made to enjoy him, and to work from that enjoyment rather than for it. We were made to enjoy our little part of the world, just as Adam enjoyed the Garden of Eden. **This truth establishes our identity, our purpose, and our destiny.** When Jesus returns, he will reverse the curse of sin and our rest will be fully redeemed and restored — we will finally enjoy what Adam did on his Day 1 (Revelation 21:1–5).

Day 2 for Adam was his first working day. He was set to work: "The LORD God took the man and put him in the garden of Eden to work it and keep it" (Genesis 2:15). This wasn't back-breaking labour — the work Adam did was before sin. Before he disobeyed God, there was no curse, and death hadn't entered the earth; he didn't have to toil to survive.

So work for Adam was not like what we experience today. His day of rest and his work were not really that different. Before sin entered, there was a blur between Sabbath and work. It would have been hard to lose his identity because of his work, as work was not cursed.

It was only after he sinned that God cursed the ground and work became difficult:

> *"And to Adam he said, 'Because you have listened to the voice of your wife and have eaten of the tree of which I commanded you, "You shall not eat of it," cursed is the ground because of you; in pain you shall eat of it all the days of your life; thorns and thistles it shall bring forth for you... By the sweat of your face you shall eat bread, till you return to the ground.'" (Genesis 3:17–19)*

Sin ruined everything and made work difficult. Work was never supposed to be this hard, but it is hard because of sin. Because we work with people who sin, work is now even harder. As anyone who has worked knows, the greatest stress of work is usually due to people.

Creation itself groans under the weight of it:

> *"For the creation was subjected to futility, not willingly, but because of him who subjected it, in hope that the creation itself will be set free from its bondage to corruption and obtain the freedom of the glory of the children of God" (Romans 8:20–21).*

This is why Sabbath isn't designed to recharge you to work — it's designed to align you with your maker. Sabbath is directional as much as it is functional. Not working one day per week will make you a better worker the other six days, but that's not its primary intention.

This pattern found in Eden was then commanded to God's people when they were led out of Egypt. God wrote it into the covenant with Israel and commanded them to keep the Sabbath, as it is *"a sign forever between me and the people of Israel that in six days the LORD made heaven and earth, and on the seventh day he rested and was refreshed"* (Exodus 31:17). **A sign — a way of remembering.**

The Sabbath was mandated when God was turning a million former slaves into a nation. They had worked without rest under Pharaoh. God was re-educating them — stop thinking like slaves and never return to working like slaves. He wanted them to remember who they were before they did anything. **The Sabbath was a national, once-per-week declaration: We are no longer Pharaoh's people; we are God's.**

Sabbath is a weekly reminder of Adam before sin and that we were made to enjoy this world and enjoy God. Sabbath reminds us each week that one day we will enjoy it to its fullest when Jesus returns: *"No longer will there be anything accursed, but the throne of God and of the Lamb will be in it, and his servants will worship him"* (Revelation 22:3). The curse on work will be lifted because there will be no sin and no consequence of sin.

Sabbath was not designed for you to achieve less. **It was designed to keep you on fire with God** — and to walk you into what he prepared for you before you were born. That is what is at stake when we skip it. Not just our productivity, not just our rest — but our alignment with the God who made us for this. What we do with the Sabbath cannot be a preference. It must be considered a matter of obedience.

WORKING GOD'S WAY

Without the Sabbath, we work for work. With the Sabbath, we work for God. We cannot work every day of the week and tell the Lord that we work for him. God instructed us to take the Sabbath, so working seven days a week is disobedience. This should be enough for us to take the Sabbath seriously. But to press the point — **when we start working every day of the week, we can't be sure if we are in God's will or not.**

Some cite Paul telling the Colossians to let no one judge them over a Sabbath (Colossians 2:16) — but his target was people making the day a test of righteousness, which is not what I am doing.

This next point won't sit well with many. But if a student studies seven days a week — which is their form of work, albeit unpaid — in order to get into the course they wanted, should they get into that course, they should not thank God as though this confirms his will. God did not ask them to study like this. When they finish their course, they will not be sure if this was God's will for them because they did not follow God's way to get there; they followed their own.

No wonder so many young people are lost, even the ones who have seemingly achieved things in life. **Achievement does not mean God's will.** So many Christians thank God for the achievements in their life; though they mean well in acknowledging God's grace, this grace falls on non-Christians too. The rain falls on the righteous and the unrighteous (Matthew 5:45) — God shows a lot of grace to everyone. **The only way to know if you are in God's will is to do things God's way.**

The ends do not justify the means. The means define the ends. The way you go about something defines what you do and who you are. The early disciples of Jesus were not called Christians. They were referred to as people of the Way — *"and asked him for letters to the synagogues at Damascus, so that if he found any belonging to the Way, men or women, he might bring them bound to Jerusalem"* (Acts 9:2). The phrase recurs throughout Acts (19:9, 19:23, 22:4, 24:14, 24:22) — these were people who followed the ways of Jesus. **We aren't called to do things the way we want; we have to do things the way he wants.**

In the Old Testament, Jacob listened to his mother Rebekah, whose ways were not righteous. She helped him trick Isaac, Jacob's father, and steal the firstborn blessing from his brother Esau (Genesis 27). What Jacob did was not the way. It might seem like he got away with it. Twenty years later he wrestled all night with a man he later called God, and would not let go until he was blessed (Genesis 32:24–30). He walked away with a limp and a new name:

> "And he said, 'Your name shall no longer be called Jacob, but Israel, for you have striven with God and with men, and have prevailed.'" *(Genesis 32:28)*

Why did Jacob wrestle and not let go? Because he wanted a blessing. Why did he want a blessing again when he had already stolen one? Because stealing his brother's blessing was never going to be enough. Perhaps something in his spirit made him think that it didn't count because he hadn't received it the right way. The blessing he was so desperate to steal, he finally received legitimately.

If we choose to work the way we want, we follow our way. And we cannot call ourselves followers of the Way.

WHEN WORK BECOMES YOUR MASTER

Work can make you feel really good. Workaholism is as real as alcoholism. Workaholics work too much not because they like work, but because it makes them feel good — just like alcoholics don't drink because they like the taste, but because of how it makes them feel.

You know work is taking over your identity when you cannot rest — because when you rest, you no longer feel like you. **The workaholic doesn't struggle to rest because they love work. They struggle because without work, they don't know who they are.** This even happens amongst Christians who spread themselves so thin they don't know how to be still before the Lord.

Work is dangerous because it can be rewarding. We were made to enjoy work and feel that sense of accomplishment because work was created by God. In his pleasure, God creates — *"And God saw everything that he had made, and behold, it was very good."* (Genesis 1:31) Because we are made in God's image and likeness (Genesis 1:26–27), we like the pleasure of creating too. Creating things can even be difficult, but strangely, the difficulty makes the outcome even more rewarding. This feeling can be addictive.

Something as utilitarian as work can become an addiction — and all addictions are bad. Just because you are addicted to something that is good doesn't mean it's okay. Paul is clear: *"All things are lawful for me, but not all things are helpful. All things are lawful for me, but I will not be dominated by anything"* (1 Corinthians 6:12). Jesus died so that we would be free — *"for freedom Christ has set us free"* (Galatians 5:1) — and that freedom includes freedom from addiction. **We need to learn to keep work as our servant, and never become servants to it.**

With work comes the lure of greater titles and prestige. Ambition is not the problem — God made us to grow, to develop, to take on more. The problem is when the pursuit of the next title becomes the thing you are living for. The hunger for more — and it's not even more money — can cause one to be addicted not just to the work, but to the desire for something more. Every graduate or junior entering an organisation dreams of having the title of specialist or manager. Once they get the next title, it soon isn't enough — they want the senior role. Soon that won't be enough either. This doesn't sound like an addiction because it can be framed as career progression, but if someone is dedicating everything to the pursuit of one thing, it sounds like addiction to me.

Let's just admit that the lure of more — more acknowledgement, more accolades, better pay, better titles, nice achievements along the way — is something we all want, but it's not something we are called to dedicate our lives to. Our dedication is to God, not to our work. **Our work must help us serve others, not be something we serve to get what we want.**

The true worth of work comes not from what work gives us, but from how our work can help others. **If we are going to be addicted, it should be in the pursuit of helping other people through our work.** Everything else — pay, titles, achievements — will just be a result of the work we do, not a goal we set out to achieve. This is a subtle difference, but it will change how others perceive you. People can sense those who do things for their own personal gain and those who are genuinely looking to help them.

When you work without Sabbath rest, you will find ungodly ways to reward yourself. But because you have no time, that compensation becomes spending — and spending that happens quickly, lavishly, and with less judgement than you would otherwise exercise. You do not eat carefully, shop carefully, or play carefully when you are exhausted. You do everything in excess because there is no time for moderation. What begins as a reasonable reward becomes a destructive pattern — and the job that was supposed to build your wealth ends up draining it.

PRACTICAL APPLICATION

Does it have to be Sunday?

No — but one day in seven, set apart. That is the command.

Sunday is still the best default, and for good reason. The early church gathered on the first day of the week in recognition of Resurrection Sunday — the day everything changed (Acts 20:7, 1 Corinthians 16:2). That practice has held for two thousand years, and there is wisdom in not abandoning it lightly. When you worship on the same day as the global church, you are joining something much larger than you or your local congregation.

But Sunday is not always possible. Shift workers, hospital staff, hospitality workers, pastors — many cannot observe Sunday consistently. That is not disobedience; it is circumstance. The principle is one day in seven, not one specific day. What matters is that the day is genuinely set apart — not a half-rest squeezed between obligations, but a full and intentional break from the rhythm of work.

Whatever day you choose, don't observe it alone. Scripture is clear:

> "And let us consider how to stir up one another to
> love and good works, not neglecting to meet

> together, as is the habit of some, but encouraging one another, and all the more as you see the Day drawing near" *(Hebrews 10:24–25).*

Sabbath was never designed as a solitary practice — it is rest taken in community, with the people who matter most to us. A day off by yourself is not the same thing. If Sunday doesn't work, find the Christians who will gather with you on another day. If you can't find them, keep looking. The Christian community should be encouraging, restorative, and energising — and if it isn't, that is worth addressing too.

The question is not which day. The question is whether you are keeping it at all.

Is it just about going to church?

Yes and no. Just as tithing is the simplest expression of giving, attending your church's Sunday service is the simplest expression of Sabbath. Keep it simple. Yes, there are many ways to experience God — a hike, nature, solitude — but these should be the exception, not the norm. Flexibility and creativity do not often foster consistency. Sabbath is a consistent reminder to keep a rhythm with God. When you limit choice, you create discipline; when you have discipline, you have structure; where there is structure, there is strength; where there is strength, there is growth. Sundays should be the backbone of your spiritual growth.

It should be the day you look forward to the most. It's the day my kids love because they don't have study, or go to training, or practise instruments. It's the day we eat out as though the Lord is buying us dinner so no one has to cook if they don't want to. It's the day we stop looking at our phones and looking for things to buy. It's a day our bodies, our minds, and our spirits can genuinely rest in God.

What if I am running a business?

Jewish leaders are known not to make business decisions on their Sabbath. They are even known to forgo deals that would require them to work on Saturday. This is a beautiful example of trusting God and his provision. Just as tithing on a $10-an-hour wage makes it easier to tithe at $100 an hour, choosing the Sabbath while the business is small makes it easier when the business is large. Decide early that you will work God's way.

At what cost? I'm not sure if I can take the risk.

As I am the Lead Pastor of my church, Sundays are technically work days even though ministry doesn't feel like work. So I take on what my kids call the "Jewish Sabbath" — from sunset Friday to sunset Saturday. But there was a time I had no Sabbath at all.

In my 30s I was working full time at a large financial institution, in the early years of planting a church, completing a postgraduate course as part of my pastoral accreditation, and raising a three-year-old with my wife expecting our second child. It was then that I realised I had lost my Sabbath. I was exhausted and I knew I needed one again.

The only way to get it back was to go part time. But a man working a four-day week in a large financial institution was unprecedented. And the timing could not have been worse — going part time would mean a 20% pay cut, in the same year my wife would begin maternity leave. We were about to go from two full-time salaries to one part-time salary and a maternity payment.

My wife's response was simple: "You need it. God will provide."

So I asked. By God's grace, the organisation said yes.

That year — and every year after — we did not dip into our savings. To this day I cannot fully explain the maths. What I can tell you is that I have held fast to my Sabbath in faith ever since and we are in better financial shape than we could have ever dreamt or achieved.

The Sabbath will cost you something. It is supposed to. The question is whether you trust God enough to pay the price.

How important is it for students?

Study is work. It's unpaid work, but it's work — and it could even be viewed as paid work in the sense that it pays back later. So for students, the priority is to create the rhythm now while the stakes are low.

Students need to face the consequences of taking a Sabbath in a low-risk environment. They need to feel the consequences of not cramming on Sunday before a Monday exam. If this results in a poor mark then they will need to bear that consequence because they should have managed their time better from Monday to Saturday. There will be seasons where the workload is genuinely heavy and grace is needed — but the habit should be the Sabbath, and the exception should be the crunch, not the other way around. The cost now is a bad mark. Later, the cost will be a job.

Apply it early, embed it early — learn to do it God's way now so you can do it his way later.

PART THREE
LETTING GO

CHAPTER 7
CLOSE TO HOME

Loosening the grip of money starts at home.

EVERY HOUSEHOLD IS DIFFERENT

Couples can benefit from having a dual income, which is potentially very helpful financially. But a single person has something no married person can ever get back: focus. The time and energy a married person invests in their spouse and family is fully available to a single person. This is a gift. Paul understood this:

> "I want you to be free from anxieties. The unmarried man is anxious about the things of the Lord, how to please the Lord. But the married man is anxious about worldly things, how to please his wife, and his interests are divided. And the unmarried or betrothed woman is anxious about the things of the Lord, how to be holy in body and spirit. But the married woman is anxious about worldly things, how to please her husband. I say this for your own benefit, not to lay any restraint upon you, but to

> promote good order and to secure your undivided devotion to the Lord." *(1 Corinthians 7:32–35)*

To be single is not a disadvantage. It is a different kind of power.

But singles, while they can exercise greater freedom as they are not bound to make decisions with a spouse, need accountability. What marriage provides — accountability, a witness, a check on decisions — singles need to build deliberately. They need a witness to encourage them. Ideally, they have a trusted friend they can share all their finances with. Short of that, it would be healthy for them to live as though they could be audited by someone who loves them.

As for how married households are structured — there is no cookie cutter approach available. A household with one income and a full-time parent at home is not automatically better for the children than a dual income household, and the reverse is equally true. Outcomes for children depend far less on income structure than on presence, intention, and the values that shape daily life. All of this can change depending on the season the family is in. **What matters is that each household is listening for what God is calling them to — and following it, without comparing themselves to the household next door.** God does not mandate any approach. He gives us choice — and asks us to steward it faithfully and judge it by its fruit.

Whether single or married, you have to take seriously when to heed financial advice and when to disregard it. **Often, Christians take money or work advice from other Christians and assume the source is biblical.** Two obvious examples are:

Young people often say among themselves, "If you are married, you lose a lot of freedom." This is poor advice. While single individuals may not have to give up their lives for a wife — *"Hus-*

bands, love your wives, as Christ loved the church and gave himself up for her" (Ephesians 5:25) — they often find themselves sacrificing their life in the unbiblical pursuit of happiness through money or work. Ultimately, every person, whether single or married, will be giving up their life, even if it's for the pursuit of idleness.

Married couples without children are often told, "It's too expensive to have children these days." Blindly listening, some then turn having children into primarily a financial decision rather than a matter of faith.

People give well-meaning thoughts, suggestions, and even advice — but sometimes it's just plain bad advice. Check if it is biblical.

ONE FLESH, ONE WALLET

When married, the two become one flesh: *"Therefore a man shall leave his father and his mother and hold fast to his wife, and they shall become one flesh"* (Genesis 2:24). They are one entity in God's eyes until one of them dies and the covenant ends. This means that when God provides, He provides to the one — the family. His provision might come through the wages of one person, but the income belongs to the married couple, not the individual. There is no "your money" and "my money" when the two are one.

NAKED AND UNASHAMED

Spending money is one of the most vulnerable things couples can do — which is exactly why so many hide it from each other. In the Garden of Eden before sin: *"And the man and his wife were both naked and were not ashamed"* (Genesis 2:25). **Married couples need to maintain that same nakedness with their finances: transparent about what comes in and what goes out.** Hiding spending is a form of covering up, and covering up destroys intimacy (Genesis 3:7–8). It is sad when the privacy of a purchase becomes more important than intimacy in a relationship.

Being transparent about finances involves real risk. It invites opinions and judgement. It can surface shame, expose insecurities, and poke at past hurt. Consider a spouse who wants to quietly support her parents financially — it feels easier to do it without telling the other. **But it is precisely through vulnerability that trust is built.** Being open, fearing the reaction, and then finding compassion instead of criticism — that is how genuine intimacy is experienced.

One danger worth naming: financial transparency can become financial permissiveness. Some couples use openness as mutual endorsement. When both partners are indulging each other's spending without accountability, transparency becomes a trap. They are no longer guarding each other; they are enabling each other. **The result is debt, financial stress, and a household that has quietly become a servant of money rather than its master.**

Having a joint account and minimising single accounts is intimacy in action. If you have a credit card, add the spouse as a secondary cardholder, even if they don't use it, so there is full transparency.

Build transparency into your life rather than having to demand it. This extends beyond finances. For example, I don't have 1:1 chats on WhatsApp with females; I add my wife in. She doesn't need to demand to see my conversations because she is in them.

LEARNING TO FIGHT WELL

Two of the most common causes of conflict in marriage are work and money. One spouse works too much; another not enough. One spends freely; another resents every purchase. One wants to support extended family; the other sees it as a drain. **These are**

not small irritations — they are fault lines, and if left unaddressed, they widen.

The solution is communication — but that answer is almost useless without a method. **Couples need to decide that they will learn to fight well.** There is a difference between a pub brawl and a boxing match. A pub brawl has no rules — the objective is to hurt the other person using whatever is at hand. Boxing has clear rules, a referee, and a defined outcome. Conflict in marriage needs to look more like boxing. Solomon puts it plainly: *"A soft answer turns away wrath, but a harsh word stirs up anger"* (Proverbs 15:1). By way of example, some rules my wife and I have agreed on — and referee each other on — are these:

1. Never use the words "never" or "always" — "you never do this," "you always do that." These sentences are almost never true, and they are attacking language designed to provoke rather than resolve.
2. Stick to the topic at hand — do not bring in past conflicts or unrelated grievances.
3. No name-calling; the person may have lied, but "liar" is a label aimed at hurting, not resolving.
4. Let the other person finish speaking — we sometimes use a physical object as a mic; only the person holding it can speak and pass it to the other person when they are finished.

The objective of every conflict is to reach a decision. If you cannot get there, agree on a time to come back to it and try again. Start and end with prayer — pray between times you talk, not for God to change the other person but to help you understand more, speak more clearly, and for God to keep you both in unity as you work through it. A couple that prays together, stays together — it's a cliché because it's true. Pray through the conflict and ask the Holy Spirit to give you a way to reach a solution. By God's grace, conflict over money and work can be worked through. Use the conflict to make your marriage stronger.

RAISING CHILDREN WITH MONEY

Do not pay children to do chores, and do not bribe them to do work. Both teach lessons you almost certainly do not intend. *"Train up a child in the way he should go; even when he is old he will not depart from it"* (Proverbs 22:6). **That training happens in everyday life, not through a classroom or a reward chart.** When children are paid for chores, they learn that work is only worth doing if someone pays for it. Unpaid work — tidying, helping, contributing to the household — becomes beneath them. That lesson follows them into adulthood.

Bribing children to perform — "if you finish this, I will buy you that" — teaches them that reward is always external. They never discover the intrinsic satisfaction of doing something well. When my eight-year-old son walked out of his AMEB (Australian Music Examinations Board) cello examination with a huge smile on his face, I told him: "You earned that smile, you earned that feeling." He had prepared four scales, three arpeggios, four exercises, three main pieces, and two extras — all from memory — plus sight-reading and an aural component. He did not do that for an ice cream. He did it because he had prepared, and the preparation paid off. That feeling is what you want your children to discover.

Children need to have the skills to be almost completely independent by the time they are eighteen. They need to be able to run a household: cook meals, do laundry, pay a bill, shop for groceries, communicate at a restaurant, and wash a car. They will not be paid for any of these things. If they cannot be consistent at home, they will struggle to be consistent anywhere else. **The foundations of work — reliability, follow-through, doing what**

needs doing without being asked — are formed at home long before they are tested in any workplace.

God's instruction for passing on these values is not a formal curriculum — it is the rhythm of daily life:

> "And these words that I command you today shall be on your heart. You shall teach them diligently to your children, and shall talk of them when you sit in your house, and when you walk by the way, and when you lie down, and when you rise." *(Deuteronomy 6:6–7)*

They need to see you tithe, so they learn that the first portion belongs to God. They need to see you keep the Sabbath and rest with you in it. They need to see you give, and they need to be taught to give. They need to see you work with integrity, and they need to understand why. Applying for a first job or starting a small business are among the best opportunities to walk alongside them through the real mechanics of money and work.

Children do not need to be forced or coerced — they need to be exposed. They do not have to have an interest in money or be passionate about work, but they do need to learn the value of both. Working with this tension requires your active, present involvement. Only you will know when to push and when to back off, when to teach and when to let them discover. That discernment cannot be outsourced.

WHEN THE CHURCH FIGHTS ABOUT MONEY

Money does not create conflict — it exposes it. What is true in marriage is true in the church. When a congregation erupts over a budget decision, a building project, or how the offering is being spent, the temptation is to treat the money as the problem. It rarely is. The financial health of the church will reflect the maturity of the church, and conflict over money will reveal any weakness. The weakness was always there — it just took a money decision to expose it.

In almost every church conflict involving money, the real issue is one of two things: how a decision was made, or what decision was made. And more often than not, it is the former. **People can accept outcomes they disagree with if they feel genuinely heard in the process.** What they cannot accept — and should not have to — is feeling as though significant decisions were made over their heads, by too few people, with too little consultation. That is not a money problem; that is a governance problem, and money simply made it visible.

This means that when money causes conflict in your church, the first move is not to relitigate the financial decision. It is to step back entirely and ask a harder question: How are decisions made here, and is that structure working? Who has a voice, and who doesn't? Are the elders or leaders genuinely consultative, or are they making large calls in small rooms? Do members feel like participants in the life of the church, or like passengers? These are organisational questions, not financial ones — and until they are addressed, the same conflict will resurface around the next budget, the next building, the next hire.

The diagnosis is almost always a people issue dressed in financial clothing. Someone feels unheard. A leader made a unilateral call that should have been shared. A group feels excluded from decisions that affect them. Money made it loud, but the wound was relational long before the figures appeared.

The path forward requires the same humility in a church as it does in a marriage — step into the discomfort rather than away from it. Leaders need to ask how members can have a louder voice — not as a concession to conflict, but as a reflection of what the church actually is. Paul describes it plainly:

> "For just as the body is one and has many members, and all the members of the body, though many, are one body, so it is with Christ... The eye cannot say to the hand, 'I have no need of you,' nor again the head to the feet, 'I have no need of you.'... If one member suffers, all suffer together; if one member is honored, all rejoice together. Now you are the body of Christ and individually members of it." *(1 Corinthians 12:12, 21, 26–27)*

Elders who lead well are not those who make the fewest mistakes with money; they are those who create the conditions for the whole community to own its decisions together.

If you are a member caught in a church conflict about money, resist the pull to make it about the money. Ask instead: what is this conflict telling us about how we are organised, how we listen, and how much we actually trust each other? The answer to that question is where the real work begins.

If you are a leader: When money becomes the flashpoint, take it as a gift. Not a comfortable one — but a gift nonetheless. Something that was hidden is now visible. Something that needed addressing has finally surfaced. Money has done you the favour of showing you where the body is weak. Treat it accordingly.

CHAPTER 8
THE ART OF SPENDING

THE PSYCHOLOGY OF SALES

Everyone loves a discount. Who wants to pay full price? Who wants to pay more than they have to? If there were a way to pay less, most of us would find it. The coupon, the sale, the end-of-season clearance — there is something chemically satisfying about purchasing something at a reduced price. Nobody leaves the shopping centre upset about the bags they are carrying. Only those who leave empty-handed are upset.

But sales are designed for the seller, not the buyer. People who put things on sale are thinking about themselves first. Sales are not acts of generosity or charity — they benefit the seller.

We are tricked into thinking the seller is doing us a favour. But they would not be selling at a discount if it were not worth their while. Sometimes sales are used to get you through the door so you spend on other things. Sales are selective — rarely is everything discounted. What is on sale is usually what the retailer is struggling to move at full price. Getting rid of slow-moving stock at a heavy discount is still profit they would not have made otherwise.

At the end of a sale, who is actually profiting? We walk away thinking we got a good deal, but often we leave with things we did not need and never planned to buy. We purchase in bulk because the per-unit price is lower, only for things to expire or never get used. We buy things because they were on sale and never open them. **We did not profit if we did not use them — we spent more than zero when we could have spent nothing.**

There are people who track sales obsessively — subscribing to every newsletter and brochure, actively hunting for bargains. Occasionally they may stumble upon a bargain for a necessity, but that is the exception. As the pursuit consumes significant time, attention, and energy for things that will generally not be necessities, the cost of the pursuit probably exceeds the savings.

Don't get enslaved by sales.

REWARD QUALITY

When we pay fairly for what others provide, we honour God who made them. Every person on Earth is made in God's image and likeness (Genesis 1:26–27). We are called to treat every person with respect and dignity — including by paying fairly for the services they provide. It is good to eat out. It is good to pay people to provide services. It is good to reward others for the value they bring to your life.

When you visit a restaurant you enjoy, the question should not be how little you can spend — it should be how well you can reward what they have given you. We would naturally take this posture if the restaurant were owned by a family member or close friend.

Apple does not run typical sales — and remains one of the most profitable companies in history. People pay what Apple demands because they have concluded the product is worth it.

Not just for the device, but for the research, technology, support, customer experience, and ecosystem. At our best, we reward good products and good service.

Tipping is an interesting case. Australians generally do not tip, but the principle behind tipping — rewarding someone who has served you well — is something Christians should hold onto. You should not need a mandatory system to make you generous to someone who has served you well.

Luke 16:9 contains one of Jesus' strangest sayings: *"...make friends for yourselves by means of unrighteous wealth..."* What we can learn from this is that we should not only reward good service but also good friends. Use your earthly resources to bless your friends.

Friendship is one of the most important assets nobody talks about. Jesus died for his friends: *"Greater love has no one than this, that someone lay down his life for his friends"* (John 15:13). Using money to buy meals, give gifts, fund experiences, or enable someone to do something they could not afford — this is what we should use our money for. Put it to work to build your friendships. This is not charity. We don't offer charity to friends. This is generosity.

VALUE TIME

Trying to save 10% on a $30 item is not the same as saving 10% on a $3,000 item. Not all savings are equal, and not all sales should be pursued with the same intensity. Sometimes it is simply better not to spend the time trying to save money — because the saving does not justify the cost. To be honest, I spent countless hours researching the right TV to buy, and after finally purchasing it, I'm not sure if the money I saved was worth it.

Moses writes: *"Teach us to number our days that we may get a heart of wisdom"* (Psalm 90:12). It is one of the most confronting verses in the entire Bible. We have a fixed number of days on this earth — not one more, not one less. Most of us live as though that number is unlimited. We spend hours hunting for discounts, researching purchases, and optimising for savings — as though time were the one resource we have in abundance. **It is not. It is the one resource we cannot replenish. Money spent can be earned again. Time spent is gone.** If Moses is right — and he is — then the way we spend our time is not a lifestyle question. It is a wisdom question.

Your time is more important than money. Your ability to be present with people is even more finite and more precious. If hunting for a bargain saves you $10 but costs you an hour — and that hour could have been spent with people you love or working on yourself — you have made a poor trade. You cannot get back lost time. More money can always be made. **You cannot recapture moments with people you love.**

Jesus did not model how to save money. **He modeled how to be present.** In every miracle, He was fully present with the person in front of him — touching them, talking with them, asking what they wanted. He was not distracted by where his next meal was coming from or whether he could find it cheaper somewhere else.

LEARNING CONTENTMENT

Capitalism functions through consumption. It relies on people spending. But we cannot blame the system for our own financial choices — blame is never a strategy. We do need to consume goods and services that others produce. **But we also need to take personal responsibility and learn the art of contentment.**

Contentment is knowing that your wants are satisfied not by material possessions or present circumstances, but by your relationship with God. David knew it when he wrote:

> "The LORD is my shepherd; I shall not want. He makes me lie down in green pastures. He leads me beside still waters. He restores my soul. He leads me in paths of righteousness for his name's sake. Even though I walk through the valley of the shadow of death, I will fear no evil, for you are with me; your rod and your staff, they comfort me." *(Psalm 23:1–4)*

Everything he needed was found in his relationship with God. **We cannot consume ourselves into contentment.** Having everything you want will not make you content — or if it does, only for a short moment before the next best thing appears.

Contentment is learnt — which means it takes time, practice, and intention. Paul explains:

> "I have learned, in whatever situation I am, to be content. I know how to be brought low, and I know how to abound. In any and every circumstance, I have learned the secret of facing plenty and hunger, abundance and need. I can do all things through him who strengthens me." *(Philippians 4:11–13)*

Often, consumption is a form of identity construction. Someone loves music, so they try to become an audiophile. Another loves cars, so they build an identity around car culture. Yet another loves cosmetics, so they build an identity around beauty. **But if our identity is embedded in our hobbies and possessions, who are we when we are not engaging with them?** We will be restless — constantly seeking out the next thing to fill the quiet.

The story of the rich man and Lazarus should serve as a warning to us all.

> "There was a rich man who was clothed in purple and fine linen and who feasted sumptuously every day. And at his gate was laid a poor man named Lazarus, covered with sores, who desired to be fed with what fell from the rich man's table." *(Luke 16:19–21)*

The rich man spent his life consuming, which led him to be consumed with himself. This was perhaps the reason he was unwilling to share anything with Lazarus, whom he stepped past every day. Obsession with oneself and indifference to others do not end well. The rich man thought he was content — but he lacked the one thing that mattered and ended up on the wrong side of Hades. Contentment is like a beautiful river that flows, not a lake that holds and goes stale.

In this way, contentment allows us to be whole even when we are not actively pursuing a passion or enjoying a possession. **We don't have to be doing in order to be** — we can enjoy being who we are, with whatever we have, in whatever circumstances we are in.

SMART SHOPPER

My friend lives by "buy once, cry once." It's a good saying — **buy quality things that will last rather than cheap things you replace repeatedly.** Did you know not all cotton is the same? Cotton varies by fibre length, which is why cheaper t-shirts start pilling — those little cotton balls that appear after repeated washing — while better ones do not. Not all fabric that says 100% cotton is the same; there are often very good reasons why something is more expensive than others.

Sadly, when old people say "they don't make them like they used to," they are right. The things made today are not built to last.

Businesses deliberately design their products to break within a set period of time — this is called planned obsolescence. The logic is simple: a product that lasts twenty years is a customer you only have once; a product that fails in three years is a customer you have repeatedly.

Computers slow down and need replacing. Batteries are glued in and cannot be replaced — by design, not by accident. Some products are not even designed to fail; they are simply poor quality from the start, using plastic where metal used to be used. Sometimes things are expensive because of branding — but other times the brand commands a premium because there is genuine quality behind it, and it is built to last. **Know the difference — and buy accordingly.**

The same principle applies to what you put on your body — and this is where cheap can be genuinely costly. Skincare, personal care, and beauty products vary enormously in quality. Many cheaper products contain ingredients — synthetic fragrances, parabens, phthalates — that are known endocrine disruptors. The endocrine system is the body's hormone system — it regulates everything from metabolism and mood to reproduction and development. Our skin is like a sponge — the exposure is direct and cumulative.

Unlike medicines, most cosmetics and personal care products in Australia do not require pre-market approval by the TGA before being sold. Processed food is regulated far less strictly than most people assume. In California, certain instant ramen products are required by law to carry the label: "Warning: Cancer and Reproductive Harm." In Australia, no such disclosure is required — you would never know. **Businesses are not required to prioritise your health — they are required to prioritise their margins.** That is simply how the system works.

My wife uses an app called Yuka — or whatever the equivalent is by the time you read this — to scan the barcode of every product we buy: food, shampoo, soap, health products, skincare. It reads the ingredients and flags anything high risk. It has changed what comes into our home. We may not care much about what endocrine disruptors do to an adult body — but we should care deeply about what they do to our children. Their systems are still developing.

Be an informed shopper, be a smart shopper. **The world does not care about you.** It cares about money.

PAY NOW OR PAY LATER

When I was in my 20s, I hated hearing from older people that "health is the most important thing." As a Christian, I thought the gospel was the most important thing. Aren't these bodies just tents that are temporary — *"For we know that if the tent that is our earthly home is destroyed, we have a building from God, a house not made with hands, eternal in the heavens"* (2 Corinthians 5:1)? Why invest in your body when it's going to die? My father died from cancer when he was 39 — he loved Jesus, and yet his body failed him. So I reasoned that older people didn't know what they were talking about and that I should just focus on everything else but my health.

It all changed when I turned 40 — when I found there was some truth to what the older people had been saying. Maybe it was because I visited my father's grave each year and saw it clearly since I was ten years old — "Died aged 39" — that in my subconscious I couldn't think beyond that year. On my 40th birthday, I was lost. When I had a quiet moment to myself, I sat with God and asked him: "Now what?" I was never ambitious, nor did I have many goals, but in that moment I had more than I could ever ask or imagine. I had hit the top of the mountain. I got no answer.

So I got in the car and visited my dad's gravesite. As always, I read the words on his tombstone and saw yet again: "Died aged 39."

There was a light drizzle and a strong breeze. My umbrella flew off to the next plot — the Jewish plot. As I ran over to pick it up, a thought came to mind: "Jews live long lives, right?" And so they did. I still remember it to this day. His name was Maurice. Died at age 100 — husband, father, grandfather, great-grandfather. It was then I asked the Lord: if you would let me live, let me live to 100. Give me 60 more years.

For some, it might be a medical diagnosis; for others, it might be seeing a loved one suffer through chronic illness. For me, it was the desire to live 60 more quality years that changed me. I had a vision that day — that on my 90th birthday, I would be healthy enough to go for a swim in the early morning at a beachside rock pool.

Most people in their 50s and 60s will tell you they wish they had taken better care of their body when they were younger. I could either have regret later, or I could do something about it now. This is when my spending on my health changed.

This is not a book about health. Peter Attia's book, *Outlive,* was transformational for me, and it is worth reading at length. Through it, I developed a plan and committed — to making a lifelong change. **Every health decision I was to make would be irreversible. I was embarking on decisions I would only make once.**

For me, that meant subscribing to a gym for access to a personal trainer and equipment — learning properly, building lean muscle where it mattered, and most importantly, not getting injured. I paid to play tennis more — my favourite sport. I wanted to bring my kids on the journey too, so I got a pull-up bar and some gymnastic rings for home. This is enough for me. Even fitting this in was hard, but I found ways to fit it.

The initial cost was small — some extra clothes and new tennis shoes. The ongoing cost is more than I ever dreamt of paying, but **this is not an expense — it is an investment in myself.** I would rather pay the price now and be healthier than I could otherwise be than pay the price later in medical expenses while being far more limited. I would rather do the work now and position myself to enjoy later than do the work later with very little to gain.

Our food costs have gone both up and down. As a family, we eat quality — high protein, whole fruits and vegetables. The grocery bills have gone up. It is strange that junk food and fast food are so cheap while good food remains so expensive — but it is a price worth paying. Where costs have come down is in how much I eat. I eat far less than I used to. I fast regularly — for my body, but also for my mind and spirit. I find that if I eat less, I am sharper and can think more clearly.

I figure that I can still get cancer or die before my 60 years are finished. But at least I will not be saying sorry to the people I love when I am lying on my deathbed. If I am lying there, I will have confidence knowing I did everything I could — and if the Lord wants me home, he is Lord and he is free to do whatever he wants.

SURRENDER

When we want something, our grip gets really strong. We obsess over it like it is the most important thing on earth — whether it is an inexpensive phone cable or a house purchase, we get really deep. And as we get deep, we get desperate. Our desperation makes us feel like it is not a nice-to-have but a must-have; that without it we will not be complete; that our life going forward will just be a compromise.

This is the grip of money. This is what it feels like when a thing — any thing — has power over you. The price tag is irrelevant. A $10 cable can own you just as completely as a $1 million house if you let it. **The grip is not about the amount. It is about the posture of your heart.**

We searched for a house during a high-demand period and were outbid repeatedly. Every auction we attended, someone else had more money. We started compromising — looking at what the listings generously called "renovator's delights," which were basically shacks sitting in swamps. We missed a wedding to attend an auction. We were that deep. The house had gone from something we wanted to something we needed — something we were convinced we could not live without. Our grip was tight and getting tighter.

After months of this, we lost steam. We lost strength. We sort of gave up — not because we wanted to, but because we were exhausted. Our grip on our new home was tight, but we didn't have the strength to hold on any longer. And so, almost without meaning to, we let go. We surrendered to the Lord and decided we would be okay with where we were. It was at that point we found a house we loved but knew we couldn't afford. My wife prayed: "Lord, if it is your will, remove the competition" — reminding herself of how God gave the Israelites the lands without them having to compete for it. On auction day, no other buyers came. We were the only bidders, and we got it for far less than we should have.

That is what it looks like to spend like you believe it's not yours. Not passive. Not lazy. We did the work — we searched, we showed up, we bid. But we had released the outcome. We were not gripping. And in the moment we held it loosely — it was like God took over.

We discovered the term "hold things of this world loosely" and hold to it as a family value and principle because we have found that there is no point having treasures on Earth. Jesus put it plainly:

> "Do not lay up for yourselves treasures on earth, where moth and rust destroy and where thieves break in and steal, but lay up for yourselves treasures in heaven, where neither moth nor rust destroys and where thieves do not break in and steal." *(Matthew 6:19–20)*

One morning we walked down the driveway to go to church only to find the car gone, just its cover on the floor. That day I was actually preaching on treasures in heaven. God had given me a real life story to tell because that's exactly how we comforted ourselves: "Lucky our treasure is in heaven — and not in cars." **Nothing in this world is worth holding onto tightly. Friend, loosen your grip.**

When you do let go — when you truly surrender — here is what God gives you in return. The Aaronic blessing in Numbers 6 tells us what it actually means to be blessed:

> *"The LORD bless you and keep you; the LORD make his face to shine upon you and be gracious to you; the LORD lift up his countenance upon you and give you peace." (Numbers 6:24–26)*

Not a bigger house. Not a better salary. You get God's face shining on you — his provision. You get his grace — the inheritance of an adopted son. You get his full attention turned toward you — his presence, his affection. And you get his peace. Jesus says: *"Peace I leave with you; my peace I give to you. Not as the world gives do I give to you. Let not your hearts be troubled, neither let them be afraid"* (John 14:27). Paul calls it *"the peace of God, which surpasses all understanding"* — a peace that *"will guard your hearts and your minds in Christ Jesus"* (Philippians 4:7). It is not the absence of difficulty. It is the presence of God in the middle of it.

This is what you have always wanted. Not the thing you were gripping. This.

CHAPTER 9
DEBT

UNDERSTANDING THE LENDER

I remember when I got approval for my first credit card. I thought to myself, "I can't believe they trust me with their money." I was happy to have access to money that was not mine. But I quickly learnt — after my first interest charge and my first late payment fee — that they lent me money so they could make money from me.

Financial institutions that lend you money want to make money from you. Banks are not charities. They exist to make a profit for their shareholders. When an institution offers you money, it does so with its own interests in mind first. It has calculated both the gain from lending to you and the risk of doing so. **Never be flattered by a bank that wants to lend to you — as affirming as it might feel.**

A good credit score feels like a badge of honour (you can check yours for free on Equifax and Experian). In reality, it is a measure of how profitable you are as a customer — and how likely you are to keep paying. The late payment fee is not a disciplinary mechanism. It is a revenue stream. The minimum repayment is not designed to help you — it is designed to extend the period over which they can charge you interest. The refinancing offer is not generosity. It resets the clock and extracts more from you.

Banks make money when you do not pay in full. They make money when you spend beyond what you can repay. They make money when you miss a payment. They make money when you refinance. This is not cynicism — it is simply how the system is designed.

How debt works has never changed: *"The rich rules over the poor, and the borrower is the slave of the lender"* (Proverbs 22:7). You never want to be in a position where someone has a claim on you.

But working with banks and borrowing money is not something to avoid. On the contrary — using other people's money is something that should be mastered. The difference between those who are trapped by debt and those who use it to build wealth is understanding: making debt work for you rather than against you.

THE TWO TYPES OF DEBT

Most personal debt falls into one of two categories: secured or unsecured.

A secured loan is when you offer something of value in return for money. The most common forms are a home loan (mortgage) and a car loan. When you take out a mortgage, you are giving the bank the legal rights to your property title in exchange for funds. If you stop making repayments — what is called defaulting — the bank can take the property. This security reduces the lender's risk, which is why interest rates on secured loans are lower.

An unsecured loan is taken out without offering security. Because the lender carries more risk, interest rates are higher and penalties for non-payment are more severe. Credit cards, personal loans, and Buy Now Pay Later (BNPL) products are all forms of unsecured lending.

There is debt that can build wealth and debt that leads to poverty. No one takes on bad debt intentionally — but it is rarely accidental either. Debt is not something you "fall into." It is something you take on, either with understanding or without it.

I do not want my children to be debt-free. I want them to understand debt well enough to take on good debt — debt that preserves or generates income — and to avoid bad debt that leaves them feeling trapped. When someone is trapped in debt, they can no longer make the decisions they want to make. They are servicing interest rather than making progress. They are not free — and the consequences of not paying back get worse over time.

Financial freedom in a biblical sense is not the absence of having to work. It is the freedom to make God-centred decisions, not money-centred ones. But this kind of freedom is not something that being debt-free just gives you — the debt-free person can be just as enslaved to money as those who are in debt.

A rule worth following: you borrow money to buy things that will either generate income exceeding the interest cost, or grow in monetary value beyond the total cost of borrowing. When someone borrows for something that does neither, they are usually trying to fill a void that money cannot fill or feeding an addiction they cannot control — whether that is gambling, compulsive shopping, or the need to project an image of wealth they do not have. No addiction is freedom.

I never want my children to ever take out a personal loan. Unlike credit cards, there is no interest-free period — interest begins the moment you draw the funds. Institutions market unsecured loans for holidays, weddings, and lifestyle purchases. **These are among the worst reasons to borrow.** Personal loans are the last resort for financing anything.

Microloans are not personal loans because their purpose is to generate income. In developing countries, they are typically small amounts borrowed from the community, based on trust, and used to invest in income-generating activity. Repayments are made over time rather than in full — and because trust is such a critical asset in a small community, borrowers are strongly motivated to repay. This is a legitimate and genuinely helpful form of unsecured lending — quite different from the short-term, high-interest microloans marketed in developed countries, which are closer to predatory lending than community finance.

Credit cards are a type of unsecured loan, but with one crucial difference — you do not have to use the credit. **In the right hands, a credit card is a powerful tool.** The single best feature of a credit card over a debit card is fraud protection: if someone makes fraudulent transactions on your credit card, the money at risk is the bank's, not yours. I once had a card fully maxed out by fraudulent transactions — I disputed them and lost nothing. You can dispute a transaction on a debit card, but the money that was stolen is yours, and you will be out of pocket until and unless the dispute is resolved in your favour.

But credit cards are also one of the most profitable products banks offer. The merchant network — Mastercard, Visa — makes money through transaction fees typically paid by retailers, which is why some pass those costs to consumers. The card-issuing bank makes its primary profit through interest and penalty fees. For the bank to be profitable on a credit card portfolio, a certain percentage of cardholders must carry a balance month to month. **The bank needs people not to pay in full to make a profit. It is designed around this assumption.**

The interest rate on a credit card balance is very high because the risk to the bank is so high. But this means if you max out your card and make only the minimum repayment, you will be paying it off for decades, depending on the size of the balance. The minimum repayment looks like a helpful feature — it is not. **It is voluntary servitude.**

The rule is simple: only use your credit card if you already have the money in your account to pay the statement in full when it is due. Not anticipated income — actual money in the account. If you use your card on the expectation of future income, it takes only a few unexpected expenses to tip you into a balance you cannot clear. Interest compounds. The cycle becomes self-reinforcing.

DEFERRED PAIN

Buy Now Pay Later (BNPL) products — Afterpay, Zip, Klarna, and their equivalents — are essentially short-term unsecured credit dressed in a more palatable format. No interest if you pay on time and seamless integration at checkout. The psychology is deliberately frictionless: by splitting a $200 purchase into four $50 payments, the perceived cost feels smaller even though it is identical.

BNPL is not inherently evil — but it is worth understanding what it is designed to do. **It is designed to reduce the psycho-**

logical resistance to spending. That is its commercial purpose. The retailer pays a fee to the BNPL provider because BNPL reliably increases average order value and conversion rates. Think of it this way — the one you are buying from (the retailer) is paying Afterpay to put you in a situation where you spend more than you intended. **You are not the customer in this transaction. You are the target.**

Used for genuine necessities where you have the funds to cover the repayments and simply prefer to spread the cash flow, BNPL is manageable. Used to purchase things you cannot actually afford, it is bad debt — with late fees and potential credit reporting consequences if you miss a payment.

THE WAY OUT

If you are carrying credit card debt or other unsecured loans and only making minimum payments, **the first thing to accept is that no one got you here but you.** Not the bank for lending, not the friend who encouraged the purchase, not the sale that triggered it. Taking full accountability for how you earn and how you spend is the first and most important step in mastering money.

The most motivating approach is usually to pay off the smallest balance first. This gives you a fast win, and that win produces motivation to tackle the next. It is not always the mathematically optimal approach — **paying off the highest interest rate first saves the most money — but the psychological benefit of eliminating a debt entirely is real and often underestimated.**

Make repayment the first priority after tithing and taxes — not the last. If you leave it as the thing you address after everything else, you will consistently find there is nothing left. If you pay repayments first and live on what remains, you will find ways to cut back that you would not have found otherwise.

Banks and credit providers will often offer hardship assistance — a repayment pause, a reduced interest rate, or a restructured arrangement — to customers who approach them proactively and demonstrate genuine intent to repay. This goodwill is typically offered once. If it is offered to you, take it seriously and use it fully.

You may also wish someone would simply pay your debt off for you. Resist that desire. **The issue is not the debt — it is what created the debt in the first place.** Clearing the balance without addressing the underlying behaviour means you will be here again. The lesson is harder and longer when you work your own way out — but that is exactly why it sticks.

Debt is often where marriage and money collide first. Sometimes one partner brings debt into the marriage, or one accumulates it after. If someone brings debt into the marriage, the other partner should know and agree to accept it as shared family debt. In marriage, the debt is always collective — the decision of the one is the decision of the other. In a good marriage, the other always knows.

The other lever is income. What can you sell? What skill can you offer on the side? What additional hours are available to you? **Making more money is itself a skill — and having a clear, urgent reason to develop it is actually a gift.** Use the motivation while it is there to build new habits, new income streams, and new financial reflexes.

GOOD DEBT

Aside from using credit cards strategically and avoiding interest entirely, there are other ways to make debt work for you. **Good debt leads to future income or an increase in wealth.** Businesses borrow money to make money — this is expected of any healthy enterprise. A loan for further education can be good debt. A loan to start a business can be good debt. A loan to expand a proven business can be good debt. An investment loan to acquire income-producing property can be good debt.

All debt involves risk. The return may be smaller than expected or may not materialise at all. This is why not everyone takes on good debt — it requires patience, tolerance for uncertainty, and the ability to delay gratification. Good debt does not feel good in the short term because satisfaction is tied to future outcomes, not present ones. **Bad debt feels good immediately. That is part of what makes it dangerous.**

Good debt is also, in many cases, tax-effective. When you borrow against an asset, the funds arrive in your account without being treated as taxable income — borrowing is not an income event. **This is a fundamental principle the wealthy use to build and hold wealth: borrow against appreciating assets, use the borrowed funds to acquire further assets, and allow the income from those assets to service the debt.** The assets grow. The borrowing is backed by increasing collateral. The cycle compounds.

The more assets you accumulate, the cheaper you can borrow — because you carry less risk for the lender. This is why access to good debt is a steep climb early in life and becomes progressively easier as your asset base grows. It rewards those who start early and stay patient.

HIGHER EDUCATION DEBT

Higher education in Australia is expensive, and government loans — HECS-HELP — make it easy to access without feeling the cost immediately. But **debt is still debt.** It needs to be paid back. The fact that repayments are tied to income and that the debt is indexed to inflation rather than bearing a market interest rate makes it more manageable than most — but it is not free money. Starting your working life with a five-figure debt that grows with inflation is a meaningful financial commitment. If you are reading this outside Australia, your student loan system will look different — but the principle holds.

For most occupations, most of what you need to do the job will be learnt on the job. Employers are not primarily hiring based on education — they use it as a filter. **What they are actually assessing in an interview is fit, teachability, resilience, and character.** An undergraduate degree, for many roles, primarily demonstrates that you can commit to something for three years and finish what you started.

This does not mean higher education is not worth it. There are professions where it is not merely valuable but essential — medicine, law, engineering, architecture — because the cost of incompetence in those fields is paid by others. **But the assumption that everyone should pursue a degree immediately after high school, without a clear sense of what they want from it, leads to significant debt for uncertain return.**

Before taking on higher education debt, consider: is there a way to get exposure to this industry first, without paying for the privilege? Can you volunteer, intern, or work in the field for a period to see what the day-to-day actually looks like? **A gap year spent working in an industry of interest will tell you more about whether you want to pursue it formally than any prospectus.** Gap years are more valuable when they are intentional — a deliberate investigation, not a holiday.

Higher education undertaken later in life, after real work experience, tends to yield a higher return. You know what questions to ask. You know which parts of the theory actually matter in practice. The debt-to-outcome ratio improves significantly when the student has context. Employers will also often fund further education for staff who have demonstrated commitment — not interest, commitment. Building strong networks and a track record in an industry can open pathways to funded study, scholarships, and research grants that simply are not available to an eighteen-year-old with no work history.

CHAPTER 10
MASSIVE COMMITMENTS

MORTGAGE 101

A home loan is not an investment in the traditional sense. Unlike shares or other assets, your home is illiquid — you cannot sell quickly without selling below market value. It is primarily a way to preserve wealth, not create it.

Yes, Australian house prices have risen significantly — but if you sell high, you have to buy high. The gain is real on paper but hard to realise. The exception is downsizing: selling a larger home for a smaller one, or selling in a high-demand area and moving to a lower-demand one. As explained earlier, the mortgage is mainly a liability — a payment obligation that limits your financial flexibility — but it can turn into an asset when you have equity you can borrow against.

"Rent money is dead money" made reasonable sense when the average house cost three times the average annual wage. At the time of writing, the average house in Australia costs more than eight times the average annual salary. **The arithmetic of renting versus buying has changed fundamentally.** Renting allows you to live in a better property, in a better location, for the same monthly outlay as a mortgage on something significantly inferior — while keeping your capital available for investments that may compound at higher rates than residential property.

That does not make renting universally superior. Home ownership provides stability, a forced savings mechanism, and the emotional weight of permanence that matters to many families. But **the instinct to own at almost any price, based on the assumption that ownership always wins, deserves more scrutiny than it usually gets.**

Wanting a house at any cost is still wanting it at any cost — appreciation doesn't justify desperation. That desire to pay any price is common — everyone stretches their budget, comforting themselves over a thirty-year mortgage: what's another ten thousand dollars? But remember when you start to get desperate — whether it be for a house, a healing, a breakthrough — **don't bargain with God.** Paul's instruction is simple: *"Do not be anxious about anything, but in everything by prayer and supplication with thanksgiving let your requests be made known to God"* (Philippians 4:6). Make your request. That is all. Don't negotiate.

Don't say, "Lord, if you give us this house, we will use it to host." I've heard couples make exactly that promise, and I told them plainly: if you're not hosting now, what makes you think you will then? They didn't love hearing it because I think they knew there was some hard truth behind it.

What makes bargaining dangerous is that it can cross into vow-making — and God takes vows seriously. Ecclesiastes 5:4–6 is worth reading slowly:

> "When you vow a vow to God, do not delay paying it, for he has no pleasure in fools. Pay what you vow. It is better that you should not vow than that you should vow and not pay. Let not your mouth lead you into sin, and do not say before

> the messenger that it was a mistake. Why should God be angry at your voice and destroy the work of your hands?"

I know this from experience. For years my son suffered severe eczema and had severe food allergies that could cause anaphylaxis. I rarely slept through the night — he would wake up scratching himself until he bled and only settled if I got up and held him. One night, exhausted, I picked him up and pleaded with God: "Please Lord, heal him. How long will you delay? How can we go to the nations like this?" The moment I said it, I knew I had made a vow. I wanted to take it back. I couldn't.

When God healed him a year later, I knew what I had to do. So when my son was eight, I took him to Thailand on a family mission trip. His job at the medical clinic was taking patients' blood pressure readings. He did it faithfully. Just to be clear, I don't believe the vow healed him — God did, out of grace. But I had made it, and so I paid it.

Don't bargain. Just ask.

YOUR MORTGAGE STRATEGY

The most dangerous pattern with mortgages is the perpetual reset. Most people buy, then after some years refinance — taking out a new thirty-year mortgage each time. The problem is that in the early years of a mortgage, most of your repayment goes to the bank as interest, not to paying down what you actually owe. You only start making real progress on the debt in the final years. If you keep refinancing every five to ten years, you are basically starting over each time — paying mostly interest while the actual debt barely moves.

The temptation is real — you have equity, the bank is willing, and the kitchen really does need replacing. But what feels like using your own money is actually taking on more debt. The progress you have made on your loan gets swallowed up into a bigger one, and you are back to square one. **You are not renovating your house with your money. You are renovating it with the bank's money** — and you will be paying for that kitchen for the next twenty years. A renovation funded by refinancing is not an investment in your home. It is an investment in your bank's profit margin.

The solution: pay your mortgage off as fast as you can. Every extra repayment you make goes straight to reducing what you owe, which means less interest over time. An offset account is one of the best tools available to Australian borrowers — it is simply a savings account linked to your home loan.

Every dollar you keep in an offset account reduces the interest you are charged each day. The more you keep in there, the less interest you pay. Most people think of a mortgage as a thirty-year commitment, but it doesn't have to be. If you put your savings into your offset instead of letting them sit in a separate account, and make extra repayments whenever you can, you will pay off your home faster than you ever thought possible. People who use their offset well often cut years — sometimes decades — off their loan without feeling like they are doing anything dramatic. The money was sitting there anyway; it just starts working harder.

Far too many people want to have the mortgage and the holidays and the renovations and the new car all at the same time. **Something has to give.** Avoid being trapped in a mortgage prison with no financial flexibility.

And when you do buy, try to buy a house. **Land is what holds value — not the building.** If your budget only stretches to an apartment, pay it off as fast as you can and use what you have built up to move into something with more land. This is how we started — paying off our first apartment within five years set us up for a house we could otherwise never have afforded. The ladder is slow, but it works. Keep your loans at a size you can comfortably manage and never stop chipping away at the debt.

Once you have built up real equity — the gap between what you owe and what your home is worth — the mortgage can become something more than just a debt to pay off. At that point, you can borrow against that equity to invest in things that generate income, like shares, an investment property, or a business. This is how a home loan transitions from a burden into a tool. Whether or how you use that equity depends on the laws at the time, your tax position, and how much risk you want to take on. **Having equity creates options.** Get proper advice from a qualified accountant before you go down this path.

FAST FINANCE

Car loans are popular and **almost universally a poor financial decision.** You pay a premium at least twice — sometimes three times.

First, you pay a premium because car loans typically require the purchase of a new or near-new vehicle, and new cars depreciate the moment you drive them off the lot. A car that is two years old with reasonable kilometres has typically lost 20 to 30 percent of its original price. The person who buys that car has saved significantly compared to the person who bought it new.

Second, you pay a premium through the interest over the life of the loan. By the time a typical car loan is fully repaid, the total interest paid can approach or exceed 20 percent of the purchase price. Very few people would consciously choose to pay 20 percent more than the listed price for a car — yet that is exactly what a car loan does.

Third, if you need to sell the car before the loan is repaid, the sale price will almost certainly not cover the remaining debt. You will need to pay the shortfall out of pocket.

There is one exception. If the car is genuinely used to produce income — a tradesperson's ute, a vehicle a business runs on — there can be significant tax benefits that offset, or even outweigh, the premiums above. The rules change year to year, so this is a conversation to have with your accountant.

For everyone else, avoid the loan. If you want to buy a car, buy whatever you want. Just buy it with cash.

CHAPTER 11
MULTIPLY

WHY INVESTING IS BIBLICAL

If you hold onto money, you will only get poorer. Inflation erodes your purchasing power every year you leave savings idle — the same dollar buys less next year than it does today. A Big Mac that cost 80 cents in 1976 costs over seven dollars in Australia at the time of writing. That is not an anomaly. That is the direction of travel for every currency in the world.

The flip side is equally true. The top 500 companies on the US stock exchange are worth roughly ten times what they were worth thirty years ago. An investor who put money across those companies and stayed invested through the volatility would have seen their capital multiply substantially over that period. This is not a guarantee of future returns. It is evidence that patient investment in productive enterprises compounds over time in a way that holding cash does not.

This is not just financial common sense — it is a biblical principle. The parable of the minas makes this explicit (Luke 19:11–27). A nobleman gives three servants sums of money to manage in his absence. Two invest it and return with gains. One buries his portion, returns it intact, and offers the excuse that he was afraid. The nobleman's response is worth close inspection: he calls this servant wicked and lazy — not simply unproductive, but wicked. The failure to put money to work is treated as a moral failure.

The key to this passage is multiplication. The faithful servants were rewarded not with equivalent returns but with significantly more — entire cities to govern. Their faithfulness resulted in multiplication. They enjoyed what they were given rather than being burdened by it. **The unfaithful servant found the nobleman's gift burdensome and therefore did nothing.** When we find money burdensome — too much responsibility, too much risk, too much temptation — we will bury it rather than grow it. That is the thing to examine and overcome.

Jesus puts it plainly: *"If then you have not been faithful in the unrighteous wealth, who will entrust to you the true riches?"* (Luke 16:11) The principle is universal — it applies to the renter, the first-home buyer, the investor, and the business owner. More is not given to those who want it. More is given to those who have proven they can be trusted with what they already have.

GAMBLING IS NOT INVESTING

Both investing and gambling involve risk and the possibility of reward. The difference is time.

If you spend your life gambling, you will end up having lost everything — because the odds are designed against you, and no one wins forever against a system built to take your money. If you spend your life investing in productive enterprises, you will end up with significantly more than you started with — because over long periods, the global economy has consistently grown, and well-run companies have consistently generated returns.

Investing is like gardening. You prepare the soil, plant the seeds, tend the growth, and wait for the harvest. You do not dig up the seeds every week to check on them. You do not abandon the garden because it rained. Gambling is like buying flowers from a market — you get the bloom immediately, but it will be dead within the week.

The temptation to speculate — to find the quick gain, to time the market, to pick the stock that will double in six months — is powerful. I know this from personal experience. I nearly lost a significant amount of money trying to trade cryptocurrency based on YouTube research. I made every mistake a naive investor makes: buying too early, selling too early, and then buying again at the top. I thought I had insight that others did not. I did not. I survived only because I did not need to sell and eventually recovered most of my capital. It was only after that experience that I read the classic books on investing — and realised within the first few chapters that I had done everything wrong. **I should have invested in myself before I invested my money.**

"Don't try to catch a falling knife" — meaning don't buy something just because the price has dropped, because it may keep dropping. "You can't time the bottom or the top" — meaning no one can consistently predict when a price has hit its lowest or highest point. These are not clever sayings — they are principles that experienced investors have learnt at cost. **The evidence overwhelmingly shows that time in the market beats timing the market.** The investor who stays invested through downturns, keeps contributing, and avoids panic-selling will consistently outperform the trader who tries to be clever about entry and exit.

IT'S SUPPOSED TO BE BORING

We are so addicted to dopamine and our baselines for happiness are so high that we will look for anything for the next rush. So when people discover any form of investing, they inadvertently look for ways to feed their dopamine addiction. This is where people who should be investing gamble, those who should be saving trade, those who should be holding sell.

Investing is not trading. The two are easily confused, but they are fundamentally different activities. Trading is time-consuming, requires constant attention, and every sale is a taxable event — triggering capital gains tax that erodes the very returns you were chasing. The more you trade, the more you pay.

Wealthy people understand something that most people never learn: the goal is not to sell. It is to hold. Patient investment in productive assets — shares in good companies, property in the right locations, stakes in businesses that generate real returns — compounds quietly over time. The investor who stays in wins. Not because they were clever, but because they were still there.

What makes this hard is that holding feels passive. When markets drop, selling feels like doing something. When prices rise, taking profit feels like winning. Both instincts are expensive. The discipline of long-term investing is largely the discipline of ignoring your own reactions — and trusting that time is doing the work you cannot see.

Good investors aim to buy assets and never sell. Assets held long enough accumulate equity — and this equity can be borrowed against to acquire more assets. No sale. No tax. No interruption to the compounding that is quietly running underneath. **This is how wealth builds on itself. Not by cashing out at the top, but by using what you have built to build more — and then holding that too.**

This is boring. It is supposed to be. **The boredom is not a sign that you are doing it wrong. It is a sign that you are doing it right.** Don't get caught up in the excitement of a transaction. The excitement waits for you twenty years later when you can barely recognise the number. Done well, that joy will belong not only to you, but to your children, and your children's children.

THE POWER TO CREATE WEALTH

Deuteronomy 8:18 records this promise: *"You shall remember the Lord your God, for it is he who gives you power to get wealth, that he may confirm his covenant."* If anything, the new covenant raises the stakes — not by promising more money, but by asking us to steward money faithfully in light of the 'true riches' God wants to entrust us with (Luke 16:11).

The question is not whether wealth creation is appropriate for Christians — the parable of the minas settles that. **The question is whether money has power over us or we have power over it.** We are called not to accumulate for accumulation's sake, but to be faithful stewards who grow what we have been given, use it to serve others, and hold it lightly enough to give it when called to.

Contentment is not the same as settling. Paul says: *"...In any and every circumstance, I have learned the secret of facing plenty and hunger, abundance and need"* (Philippians 4:12). This is not an instruction to be content with little. It is an instruction not to complain — in either direction. **Contentment in plenty means you do not become defined by your abundance. Contentment in want means you do not become paralysed by your scarcity.**

Having little is an opportunity for God to multiply — as he did when five loaves and two fish were placed in his hands: *"And they said to him, 'We have only five loaves here and two fish.' And he said, 'Bring them here to me.'... And they all ate and were satisfied.*

And they took up twelve baskets full of the broken pieces left over." (Matthew 14:17, 20) Having much is an opportunity to give generously and make a significant, long-lasting impact. **Both are faithfulness when God is in them.**

Remember, the purpose of wealth is not for you. Jesus warns us in Luke 12 with a principle that acts as a counterweight to the multiplication principle. The rich man's failure wasn't that he built barns or stored grain — this is, in fact, good stewardship. His failure was the assumption that his abundance was for his own comfort. *"...Soul, you have ample goods laid up for many years; relax, eat, drink, be merry"* (Luke 12:19). God calls him a fool that very night. **The warning isn't against building wealth; it's against hoarding it and treating the future as secured.** Invest, yes — but hold it lightly. The barn might be full tonight and empty by morning, and you have to be okay with that. Life is not about the barn.

Joseph is one of the best examples of a wealth creator and preserver in all of Scripture (Genesis 37–50). He managed someone else's wealth faithfully before he managed his own. He planned across a seven-year horizon. He saved during abundance rather than spending it. He distributed generously in scarcity. And he understood that his gifting was not for his own benefit but for the blessing of others — including the very brothers who had wronged him. Joseph demonstrates that character precedes wealth, stewardship precedes ownership, and that God builds faithfulness in us through hardship so we can be fruitful in the harvest.

CHAPTER 12
JUST LIKE GOD

WHY WE GIVE

Because God is a giver.

We have been made in the image and likeness of God. **When we give, we are most like our Maker.** The reason we feel good when we give is that we were wired this way. God wired us to experience the same joy he experiences when he gives. Jesus endured the cross for this very reason: *"looking to Jesus, the founder and perfecter of our faith, who for the joy that was set before him endured the cross, despising the shame, and is seated at the right hand of the throne of God"* (Hebrews 12:2).

Giving was designed to make us glad. If we give reluctantly, we miss the point — and we miss the gladness that giving is supposed to produce. God loves a cheerful giver (2 Corinthians 9:7). **It is much easier to give cheerfully if you truly believe that what you are giving was given to you by God to give in the first place.**

"When he asks us to sacrifice, he has already prepared the offering." My aunt told me this, recalling the story of God preparing the

ram for Abraham (Genesis 22:13–14). When God asks us to give — even to sacrifice — we should be excited, because it means he has prepared the gift for us to give. How can you see the hand of God? You can see it when you give.

You can end up with a lot of money and be far from God, or be wealthy and be very close to God. The difference between the two experiences will be in the giving.

GIVING AS AN ACT OF FAITH

Giving with sacrifice is an act of faith. Faith is the primary currency of the kingdom. When the widow gave her two copper coins, Jesus said she had given more than anyone else — because she gave with the greatest faith (Mark 12:41–44). The widow of Zarephath gave Elijah her last meal. When he asked her for food, she told him she had only enough for one final meal for herself and her son. His response was a command of faith:

> "Do not fear; go and do as you have said. But first make me a little cake of it and bring it to me, and afterward make something for yourself and your son. For thus says the LORD, the God of Israel: The jar of flour shall not be spent, and the jug of oil shall not be empty, until the day that the LORD sends rain upon the earth." *(1 Kings 17:13–14)*

She obeyed — and the flour and oil did not run out (1 Kings 17:15–16). Both widows gave everything they had to live on. **Dollar value is not the measure. Faith is.**

We must constantly look for ways to give with sacrifice. It is perhaps the simplest act of faith available to us that has significant kingdom impact.

Our giving needs to cost us something. When David purchased Araunah's threshing floor to build an altar, Araunah offered to give it to him for free — the oxen, the wood, everything. David's response is the heartbeat of this chapter: *"I will not offer burnt offerings to the LORD my God that cost me nothing"* (2 Samuel 24:24). He paid full price for everything. The sacrifice is sometimes not the money itself — it is the feeling of insecurity you bring to God when you give. **That feeling of not being sure is itself an offering. You cannot give that for free.**

We are all wired to want to receive something when we give. We give presents because it feels good to see the reaction. We get something in return when we cook for others, pay for someone's meal, or invest in a friendship. God designed us this way — there is no need to fight it. What God says throughout scripture is: let me reward you. When you give so that God can reward you, your giving not only makes you more like God — it brings you closer to him. That reward may not be money. **If you give to get more money, you are demonstrating love for money, not love for God.**

GIVE TO YOUR CHURCH

We mock God when we do not sow into the church while hoping to reap from it. Paul is blunt: *"Do not be deceived: God is not mocked, for whatever one sows, that will he also reap"* (Galatians 6:7). This is like a farmer who expects a large harvest while refusing to invest in seed, fertiliser, or water. You cannot reap where you have not sown. Many people say they love their church but have invested almost nothing in it financially. Tithing does something in your spirit beyond the transaction — it forms roots, it creates ownership, it ties you into a community in a way that attendance alone never will.

What if every member of the church gave their tithe regularly? Some would say it is too much for the church to handle. And they are right. The saying "absolute power corrupts absolutely" was made famous after Lord Acton used it in 1887 when he was addressing not only governments but the church specifically. The church is not immune. **So churches must change — as the giving gets bigger, the governance needs to evolve so that it prevents corruption.**

From the day my church opened a bank account, I made a decision not to be a signatory or have any access to its transactions. I did not want the temptation of financial power to come anywhere near me. The way our church is structured, all major financial decisions are made by the members in quarterly meetings throughout the year. Minor decisions are delegated to a team of elders who must reach a majority vote before acting. There are almost no financial decisions the pastor can make alone.

I believe most of my members tithe. I cannot be certain as I have no access to our banking records — but based on our overall giving figures, the numbers suggest most of them are. This enables our church to do whatever God calls us to do. **Imagine if all Christians gave their full tithe to their church. What change would it bring? What would happen in God's kingdom that is otherwise not happening?** I have no doubt the church would be able to do far more than anyone could ask or imagine.

PAY YOUR PASTOR WELL

This is one area of giving that most books on money avoid — likely because many of the authors are pastors themselves. I'll say it because it needs to be said: pay your pastor well.

Paying your pastor well is not about making you feel guilty. It is about a simple economic reality.

Your pastor does not operate in a standard competitive labour market. You are free to find a better-paying job — you can negotiate, walk away, start a business, or change industries. The market sets a floor under your income because your skills are portable. Your pastor's are not — or at least, not in the same way. They have given themselves to one community, one call, one place. The moment they are seen to be shopping around, their credibility erodes. They cannot leverage a competing offer. They cannot threaten to leave without it costing them everything they have built. **The competitive labour market that protects your income has almost no reach inside a church.**

This means the congregation holds a power over the pastor that neither party usually names. The congregation sets the price. And because pastoral ministry is a calling rather than a career, most pastors will stay even when the price is insulting — not because they are foolish, but because they love their church and they love what God has called them to.

Paul addresses this directly. In 1 Corinthians 9, he walks through the logic carefully: soldiers are not expected to fund their own campaigns, and farmers eat from their own harvest. His conclusion is clear: *"the Lord commanded that those who proclaim the gospel should get their living by the gospel"* (1 Corinthians 9:14). He cites the same principle twice in his letters. First from the Old Testament: *"You shall not muzzle an ox when it treads out the grain"* (Deuteronomy 25:4) — and then applies it directly to gospel workers: *"The laborer deserves his wages"* (1 Timothy 5:18). And to those who receive teaching, he is equally plain: *"Let the one who is taught the word share all good things with the one who teaches"* (Galatians 6:6). The New Testament is not shy about this.

Paul himself chose not to take support from the Corinthians — but he is clear it was a choice, not a right they had over him. He waived it for his own reasons. The fact that he waived it does not mean your pastor should. Most pastors do not have Paul's tentmaking income. Many are quietly carrying financial stress they will never mention from the pulpit, because they don't want to appear needy to the people they are leading. That is a lonely and undignified position to put someone in.

A pastor's decision not to pursue outside income does not reduce the congregation's obligation. And even if they do have outside income, the church should still be supporting them — as an act of honour. Paul uses the word "double honour" for elders who lead and teach well: *"Let the elders who rule well be considered worthy of double honor, especially those who labor in preaching and teaching"* (1 Timothy 5:17). Double. Not adequate. Not fair. Double.

In some traditions, pastoral pay is set by a denomination or governing body rather than the local congregation. If that is your context, the principle still applies — advocate through whatever channels you have. The obligation does not disappear because the decision sits elsewhere.

One more thing. Your pastor is trying to learn about money in the same broken world you are — but without your resources, your network, or your freedom to experiment. The best thing a congregation can do is not simply pay their pastor enough to survive, but enough to thrive — to invest, to give generously themselves, to model the very principles they preach.

A pastor who has never had enough to invest cannot teach about stewardship from experience. Pay your pastor well enough to learn about money with you, not just teach it to you.

If you hold a position of financial leadership in your church — as an elder, deacon, or finance committee member — you carry particular responsibility here. Pastoral pay reviews rarely happen, and you should save your pastor from having to raise it themselves. It is very unlikely they will ask. **Make it your job to ask on their behalf.**

Before you meet, ask not just whether the salary is adequate — but whether it is honourable, and whether it has kept pace with the cost of living.

When you sit down with your pastor, ask whether they have been able to save, to give, to invest. These are not intrusive questions. They are the questions of a congregation that takes seriously its responsibility to those who serve it.

If the salary cannot move, there are still ways to honour your pastor well. Contribute generously above the minimum superannuation guarantee — this is one of the most practical and tax-effective ways a church can build long-term security for someone who may never build it themselves. If your church has the capacity, go further — invest on their behalf. Set up a structure that means their future is not entirely dependent on what they could save from an insufficient wage. **Do the financial work for them that their calling has made it hard for them to do for themselves.**

You want your pastor to stay. You want them to lead without fear. You want them to preach without compromise. None of that comes free. Pay them with double honour — and let that payment be an act of faith, not just a budget line.

GIVING TAXES GRACIOUSLY

Paying taxes is a form of giving. I have a relative who owns his own business and pays more tax than most of his peers. To him, it is simply allowing the poor to benefit from his success through the government's redistribution. He sees taxes as a form of social welfare — charitable giving by another name. And he is not wrong. In Australia, a significant portion of the federal budget goes directly to social welfare — aged care, disability support, Medicare, public housing, unemployment benefits, and family payments.

When you pay tax in Australia, you are not simply funding bureaucracy. You are funding the safety net that catches the people who have fallen. You are the reason someone received medical treatment they could not afford, or a pension that kept them from destitution, or a payment that kept a family fed while a parent looked for work. **That is not a small thing. That is the gleaning law in action** — but in my relative's case, administered by Centrelink.

Doing everything possible to minimise every cent of tax is not the posture God seeks. God commanded Israel:

> "When you reap the harvest of your land, you shall not reap your field right up to its edge, neither shall you gather the gleanings after your harvest. And you shall not strip your vineyard bare, neither shall you gather the fallen grapes of your vineyard. You shall leave them for the poor and for the sojourner: I am the LORD your God." *(Leviticus 19:9–10)*

This was God-mandated social welfare, designed to keep Israel mindful of its own story: they were once Pharaoh's people, without land, without means. Ruth lived this principle firsthand — a foreign widow with nothing, she came to glean from the edges of Boaz's fields to survive. Boaz, honouring the law, went further than the minimum: *"Let her glean even among the sheaves, and do not reproach her. And also pull out some from the bundles for her and leave it for her to glean, and do not rebuke her"* (Ruth 2:15–16). **God's people are to be kind to those without, because they remember what it was to be without.**

God returns to this theme repeatedly throughout the Old Testament — remember. Remember who you were. Remember what I did. *"You shall remember that you were a slave in Egypt, and the LORD your*

God redeemed you" (Deuteronomy 15:15). *"You shall remember that you were a slave in the land of Egypt"* (Deuteronomy 24:22). He says it not once but again and again, because Israel kept forgetting. Memory was meant to produce generosity — you were without, so you give to those who are without. You were poor, so you do not despise the poor. You were a foreigner, so you welcome the foreigner.

Paying taxes is a form of that same remembering. There was a time when you did not earn enough to be taxed. There was a time when you had nothing the government wanted. Now you do — and that is evidence of God's provision. The tax bill is not a punishment. It is a reminder. You have been brought out. You have been given more than you once had. **The appropriate response is not to fight to keep every cent, but to give — as God gave to you — with an open hand.**

There is another posture worth naming — those who structure their lives around minimising tax through residency. Some move countries deliberately to become tax residents in low-tax jurisdictions. Some live nomadically, spending just enough time in each country to avoid being taxed anywhere significantly. The financial logic is understandable. The theological logic is harder to defend.

God's vision for his people was never nomadic permanence. The Israelites wandered — but the wilderness was never the destination. The promised land was. God gave them land because land means roots, community, responsibility, and belonging. **You cannot love your neighbour if you do not have one.** You cannot be part of a body if you are never in the same place long enough to be known. The promise of land was not just about property — it was about the kind of settled, rooted life that makes genuine community possible.

Some argue that an online presence is the modern equivalent of establishing yourself — and there is something to that. But behind many of these nomadic arrangements is a life that is deeply displaced. Not rooted in a neighbourhood. Not accountable to a local church. Not known by anyone who will show up when things go wrong. **It's important to ask if your tax strategy aligns with God's strategy for you.**

Jesus paid his taxes — and commanded his disciples to give to Caesar what belonged to Caesar (Matthew 22:21). Paul echoes this: *"Let every person be subject to the governing authorities. For there is no authority except from God, and those that exist have been instituted by God"* (Romans 13:1). The fuller argument runs through verse 7 — honour the governing authorities, for they are God's servants. **We have limited time on this earth and finite energy. Spend it on things worth fighting for.**

Worship the Lord when you pay your taxes. It means you have an income. There is no reason for grumbling when you pay taxes — it is simply evidence that God has provided for you in ways the world itself can verify.

SAVING TO GIVE

It is easier to give when you have planned for it. Jesus commands: *"Give to everyone who begs from you, and from one who takes away your goods do not demand them back"* (Luke 6:30). We know this is a hard commandment. But we can make it easier by setting money aside before we are asked — by designating funds as "not mine" before the need arises.

Most people encounter a need — or a request for money — and respond with flight, freeze, or fight. They look away, they stall, or they find a reason why this particular need is not their responsibility. It looks like indifference. Often it is fear — fear that giving will cost them something they cannot afford to lose, or that God is about to ask them to cough up more than they are ready for. **That fear is a signal. It tells you that money still has power over you.** Saving to give breaks that power. When you pre-designate money as belonging to others before the need arrives, the decision is already made. You are not being asked to give — you are simply releasing what was never really yours.

I have people I love who are not good at financial management. I cannot trust them with a lump sum — some are too generous and will give away what I have given them before they need it themselves. So I save on their behalf. When the need comes, I can respond without the decision costing me what it might otherwise, if I had to produce a large sum at once. **Saving for others makes generosity more accessible.**

Sometimes the giving needs to be anonymous — and saving in advance makes that possible too. I remember wanting to bless a relative — let's call her Aunty — but knowing she would never accept money directly from us. She was older, a relative, and her dignity mattered more than our gesture. So we gave the money to my mother-in-law and told her that someone from our church had asked us to pass it on. My mother-in-law tried to find out who. We kept our secret. We actually watched her give it to Aunty — and Aunty received it with her dignity intact. That giving was only possible because the money had already been set aside. We were not scrambling to find it — we were simply releasing what had already been designated.

Set up a separate account — call it whatever you want: seed fund, giving tree, charity, missions. Contribute a small amount regularly. A missions fund is for going yourself or sending others; a charity fund is for responding to needs as they arise. Both serve a different purpose and both are worth having. When you see a need, or when the opportunity to go on a mission arises, you can respond with integrity. Rather than fundraising from others while having contributed nothing yourself, you can honestly say that you have been saving towards this.

NOT YOUR PROBLEM

We often worry about whether the beggar will spend what we give on alcohol, or whether the organisation will squander our donation, or whether the person we have lent money to will use it irresponsibly. These are legitimate questions. **But they are not sufficient reasons to stop giving altogether.**

The Good Samaritan did not know who the man in the road was. He may have been a criminal. The Samaritan helped anyway — and then did something remarkable:

> "A man was going down from Jerusalem to Jericho, and he fell among robbers, who stripped him and beat him and departed, leaving him half dead... But a Samaritan, as he journeyed, came to where he was, and when he saw him, he had compassion. He went to him and bound up his wounds, pouring on oil and wine. Then he set him on his own animal and brought him to an inn and took care of him. And the next day he took out two denarii and gave them to the innkeeper, saying, 'Take care of him, and whatever more you spend, I will repay you when I come back.'" *(Luke 10:30, 33–35)*

He had no way of knowing what he would be charged. He could have been scammed. He gave with no control over the outcome and no guarantee of honest accounting. In some sense, he gave irresponsibly — and Jesus held him up as the model. **The primary purpose of our giving is to shape us — not the recipient.** What the innkeeper charged, what the beaten man did next

— none of that was the Samaritan's concern. **How your giving is used is not your problem. It never was.**

This is how God gave to us: *"For God so loved the world, that he gave his only Son, that whoever believes in him should not perish but have eternal life"* (John 3:16). He gave without demanding a particular response. We are free to receive it, ignore it, or misuse it. God is not responsible for the wolves who exploit his gift. We are not responsible for the salvation of someone who rejects the gospel we share with them. We give. The rest is between the recipient and God.

It is important to note that learning to receive is as much a spiritual discipline as giving. Pride often disguises itself as self-sufficiency. The refusal to let others pay, to accept a gift without deflecting, or to be on the receiving end of someone's generosity — that is not independence. It can be a sign of pride. You have to be okay with letting someone have power over you and receiving it as love.

If we are not able to receive graciously, it probably mirrors how we relate to the free gift of grace — we refuse it, reject it, or try to earn it instead. **Not receiving exposes our heart condition.** If you struggle to receive, get your heart checked. Not as a crisis — as a discipline. Many of us carry patterns around money, generosity, and receiving that were formed long before we had any say in the matter. A trusted pastor, a wise friend, or a Christian counselor can help you see what you cannot see yourself. There is no weakness in that. **The weakness is in staying stuck.**

OUR JOURNEY

Our first mission fund was just 1% of our income. I didn't even create a new bank account — I just tracked it in Excel. We used it to give.

I cannot share too much about our giving because we want our reward to be in heaven — *"But when you give to the needy, do not let your left hand know what your right hand is doing, so that your giving may be in secret. And your Father who sees in secret will reward you"* (Matthew 6:3–4).

What I will share is that for all that we have given away, we have never been at a loss, nor have we ever regretted the decision — even when the decision was made in difficult financial circumstances. As I've said earlier, it's better not to vow at all — but if you ever make a pledge or a promise, keep it. God is not pleased with those who make a vow and do not follow through — *"When you vow a vow to God, do not delay paying it... it is better that you should not vow than that you should vow and not pay"* (Ecclesiastes 5:4–5). **You might not gain from following through, but you have too much to lose not to.**

There is a verse where Jesus says that if someone asks you, you should not refuse: *"Give to the one who begs from you, and do not refuse the one who would borrow from you"* (Matthew 5:42). It is one of his most confronting commands. I remember catching a train to a wedding — unusual for us, as we would normally be driving. We were all dressed up, the whole family. I happened to be carrying cash that day — a few fifty-dollar notes, just in case. A young man came into the carriage and said, quietly and apologetically: "I'm so sorry. I'm so sorry to disturb you all. But I desperately need some money right now. Can you please give to me?"

As expected, everyone looked away without looking away. I had three responses in less than three seconds. First: I don't want to give it — my instincts about who was asking were not generous. Second: I have nothing smaller than fifty dollars. Of all the days to be carrying cash. Third: I have to obey. So in front of my wife and children I pulled out the fifty and handed it to him. "God bless you." The train pulled into the next station and he ran out. Then he turned back, pressed his face to the glass, and shouted through the door: "Thank you. Thank you" — with the biggest, most genuine smile I have seen on a stranger's face. We were prepared to give. I obeyed. And my children saw it. I couldn't have planned it if I tried.

If someone asks you for money, give it — we have found it better not to loan it. Especially amongst family, don't lend money — just give it if you have to. **Don't let money break relationships. Giving money doesn't break relationships. Bad debts do.**

That said, when the person asking is someone you love and the amount is significant — significant enough that it could become a pattern — there is wisdom in being honest. **"I'll give it to you, but I want you to know this is the last time I can"** is not unkind. It is generous and honest at the same time. It protects the relationship from quietly becoming a transaction. It also protects the person you love from developing a dependency that will eventually cost them more than money. Saying it once, clearly and without shame, is an act of love — not a withdrawal of it.

We have never given for the sake of what others think of us. We give because our giving is between us and God. Some people give more than they should because of pride — because they want the recipient to think well of them. Some give hoping to get something back. This is not how to give. **Give because you want to, and give for the sake of giving — not expecting anything,**

not even a thank you. Some people get bitter when the person doesn't say thank you. You shouldn't. Their rudeness, their lack of gratitude, their inability to acknowledge what was given — that is not your problem. It is theirs.

CONCLUSION

As you have read, the principle of letting go is simple but the application is hard. Much like all things in God's kingdom — *"For the gate is narrow and the way is hard that leads to life, and those who find it are few."* (Matthew 7:14). Decisions around money and work are God's platform for discipleship — forming us and making us more like his Son. The Son of Man lived his life as a servant, not a master, and as a son, not as a slave. He navigated money and work perfectly to live the perfect life as an example for us to follow.

If you feel behind or your situation or circumstance is tough, remember that in Christ, hardship is never the end of your story — we are more than conquerors through him who loved us (Romans 8:37).

The Love of Money

Money is not evil. The love of money is: *"For the love of money is a root of all kinds of evils. It is through this craving that some have wandered away from the faith and pierced themselves with many pangs"* (1 Timothy 6:10). The difference is not semantic — it is everything. Money in the hands of a servant of God is a surgical tool for the kingdom. The same money in the hands of someone who loves it becomes a chain.

The tithe is what keeps money in its place, not because giving ten percent makes you righteous, but because it keeps you free — free from the love of money. You need to ensure money does not have a grip on you, but you also need to learn to loosen your grip on money. No other strategy sets you free like tithing, because no other strategy throws you into the mercy of God. Every other strategy starts to look like self-help.

Use money as a tool. Make it serve you. Make it work hard. Do not let it tell you what to do — only God can do that. Do not make decisions because you have a lot of it or because you have little; make faith-based decisions despite what you have. Enjoy what money can do for you — that is still making money serve you. But when you find yourself being self-indulgent, self-serving, or just plain selfish with money, bring it back into line by giving.

Make money your servant.

Work as Worship

Work and income are not the same thing. They have been confused for so long — particularly in our culture, where identity is built around vocation and salary — that separating them takes deliberate effort. The framework we have been building through this book rests on this distinction.

God is the source of income. He is your security. He alone gives stability. The employer is a channel, not the source. The investment return is a channel, not the source. When you hold fast to this, everything changes — the way you respond to a pay rise, the way you respond to redundancy, the way you respond to a season of thin returns.

Consider the life of Jesus. He spent thirty years in Joseph's household, working as a carpenter (Mark 6:3), and only three in what we would call 'ministry.' Luke's commentary on the thirty years is brief: Jesus *"increased in wisdom and stature and in favor with God and man"* (Luke 2:52). That is the fruit of faithful, ordinary work done in the presence of God — and the fruit we can enjoy through our ordinary work.

The fruit was not the product of what Jesus built with wood. It was the product of how he went about it — submissive, present, faithful to what was in front of him. When the Father spoke from heaven at his baptism: *"This is my beloved Son, with whom I am well pleased"* (Matthew 3:17) — Jesus had not yet preached a sermon or performed a miracle. God was pleased with thirty years of Jesus as a carpenter's son.

This should cause us to repent — to change our mind on work. Your work as a nurse, a teacher, a tradesperson, a barista, a business analyst — it is not less valuable than ministry work. It is not secular while ministry is sacred. There is no sacred-secular divide in the kingdom. What matters is whether you are working as though God gave you the work to do.

Your theology of work should shape work as a platform to serve. This is how work itself can be worship. If work is worship, then we would not expect to be paid — no one gets paid to worship. But God in his generosity provides through it. Therefore, any income we receive becomes a grace from God.

Never work for money.

Holy Pattern

When the Israelites were slaves, they worked seven days a week. When God commanded them to remember the Sabbath and keep it holy, he was ensuring that once a week they would be reminded of who they were — not slaves:

> "Remember the Sabbath day, to keep it holy. Six days you shall labor, and do all your work, but the seventh day is a Sabbath to the LORD your God. On it you shall not do any work, you, or your son, or your daughter, your male servant, or your female servant, or your livestock, or the sojourner who is within your gates. For in six days the LORD made heaven and earth, the sea, and all that is in them, and rested on the seventh day. Therefore the LORD blessed the Sabbath day and made it holy." (Exodus 20:8–11)

He was giving them a new identity and building into their weekly rhythm a structure that would keep them from drifting back to their former identity.

Christians should aim to keep at least one day of the week genuinely separate. Whether Saturday, Sunday, or a combination — there should be twenty-four hours where you intentionally engage in activity that reminds you of who you are. This is why working on Sundays should be avoided where possible. If your work currently requires it, treat that as temporary and set a clear horizon for when you would be willing to walk away if it continued.

Keeping the Sabbath involves cost — and that cost is part of what makes it worship. If attending church cost nothing, it would not be much of a sacrifice. Missing the beach or the clearance sale to keep the Sabbath is an opportunity cost. That cost is the offering.

Part of Sabbath rest is disconnection — unplugging from work and from the noise of the world. A day where you do not talk about work, do not check email, do not plan purchases or obsess about finances. It is a separate day, different from all others, where your attention goes to God and to the people closest to you. The Sabbath needs to be about your church, your family, and your friends. These are the most important people in your life, and having them around you weekly is a reminder of why you work and how you should work.

Remember who you are.

The Foundation

The Sabbath and the tithe are not theoretical commitments — they are weekly and monthly practices that are the foundation for everything else to be built on. The Sabbath is the weekly declaration that you are not defined by your productivity and a surrender to God's ways. The tithe is the monthly declaration that your income is not yours and a surrender to God's provision.

These two practices, maintained consistently over a working life, will do more to protect you from the love of money than any financial strategy. They are the spiritual infrastructure beneath all the practical guidance in this book. Without them, the practical guidance becomes self-improvement. With them, it becomes discipleship.

A Final Word

Neither work nor money should be your master. There is only one master worth working for.

The goal was never to be debt-free or financially free in the world's sense. The goal is to be free from the love of money — free to make God-centred decisions, free to give generously, free to rest without guilt, free to work without being defined by your output.

Jesus is Lord. Money and work are tools. Let go, and live.

PASTORAL WORD

So many Christians are living enslaved to money — and what makes it so heartbreaking is that they are choosing to stay. Jesus has already unlocked the prison door. The key has been turned. The cell is open. And still, people remain inside.

For some, it is because they cannot yet imagine life on the other side. The freedom is real, but it has never been tasted, and it is hard to trust what you have never experienced. If that is you, this is an invitation to take God at his word — not because you feel ready, but because he has already proven himself faithful. Freedom from the grip of money is waiting. You only need to take one step outside the door.

For others, the prison has become home. There is a strange comfort in what is familiar, even when what is familiar is a cage. Some people know the door is open and choose to stay anyway — because the certainty of captivity feels safer than the uncertainty of freedom. Money has become not just a master but a companion. The love of it has become the shape of their daily life, and to let it go would feel like losing themselves.

I earnestly long for every person who has read this book to make the bold decisions that follow from what they have learnt — and not look back. Not to become obsessed with money, but to master it. Not to chase wealth, but to steward it. Not to love what money can buy, but to love the One who gives us the power to earn it. To desire mastering money as a way to follow the Master — our Lord Jesus Christ.

That is the whole point. That has always been the whole point. Let's follow him together.

So if the Son sets you free, you will be free indeed.
(John 8:36)

ABOUT ME (SO FAR)

I am so grateful my family migrated from South Korea to Australia when I was 4. Sadly, my father died when I was 10, but my mother did a great job raising my brother and me as a single mum. My mum did the best she could, and she gave us every opportunity to thrive. I learnt hard work and resilience from her.

I have always loved economics — particularly macroeconomics. It was my favourite subject in high school and I did very well in it. It was in high school that I got my first job at 14, earning $4.61 per hour, one day a week, 4 p.m. to midnight. Yes, I tithed $8 — rounded up — every fortnight.

During university, I worked as a private tutor in the evenings, teaching everyone from primary school kids to HSC students. Most of my work came through a free advert in a Korean magazine you could pick up at Korean grocery stores. I am amazed to this day that anyone called me. At my peak, I had nine students and was earning around $360 a week, getting to most of them by public transport or borrowing my mum's car. I studied a Bachelor of Commerce alongside it — economics by day, tutoring by night.

My first corporate job was as a Business Analyst — another way of saying Microsoft Office specialist. I got particularly good at Excel because the company was small, and everyone relied on me for anything on a spreadsheet. Eventually, I learnt VBA and built macros — basically bots that did my repetitive work in seconds instead of thirty minutes. This was where I learnt that I loved to find efficiency. I was paid $40,000 a year, and I was grateful. After tithe, I paid the rent on the house my family was living in, covered my expenses, gave myself a small allowance, and gave the rest to my mother — and occasionally my brother.

I got married at 24, around job 2. I think the fact that I was paying rent and earning a decent wage gave me enough confidence to think I could do it. Or maybe it was faith. Or maybe it was really, really wanting to get married. My wife nearly didn't marry me because I told her I intended to become a pastor — there was about a month during our engagement where she went MIA, and there was radio silence. Pastors were never known for an easy financial life, nor could I guarantee one. Fortunately for me, she said yes — and fortunately for her, her fears about our finances have never materialised. From the first day of our marriage, she also said yes to tithing — not because I asked her to, but because she chose to. That yes has shaped everything since.

When we got married, we purchased a small two-bedroom apartment west of Parramatta — nowhere near anything at the time. Not only did I buy my first property, I also bought my first car.

Over the next five years, I worked four jobs, each with a significant pay increase. I played the game — building skills, gaining experience, moving on. One of the biggest lessons came from job 3, where I was working for someone I couldn't stand. The money had blinded me to the manager in the interview. I learnt then that I needed to be interviewing my next manager as much as they were interviewing me. Since then, I have never wasted an opportunity to ask questions at the end of an interview, and I have never taken a job just for the money.

Job 4 ended with our first major financial decision as a couple. We decided as a family that I would study full-time for my ministry degree. My wife became the primary breadwinner—she had only just started her first full-time job, so her pay was modest. I received a small monetary gift from the church twice a year; nothing that could be called a salary. We recorded every penny we earned and spent and somehow, at the end of every year, we hadn't touched our savings—in fact, they grew. That season cemented my wife's view of tithing: when you use money God's way, you get a God outcome.

I finished the three-year degree in two years — loading up summer and winter school — and came out the other side with a Master of Divinity. A big part of me was never happy with my wife being the breadwinner, so I worked hard to finish quickly.

Then job 5. During that time, I became the first person in the entire organisation—one of the biggest in the world — to work a compressed work week, and later the only one permitted a four-day part-time arrangement, well before any of that became normal. I even worked a three-day week in a role I pitched directly to the COO. I created the job description and even the position title. All these experiences led me to believe that God was providing me with ways to remain and for the financial institution to foot the bill for my church plant.

My 30s were transformative: we planted a church, had our first child, and bought our first house. We kept the apartment as an investment — its location near a major hospital made it easy to lease. Then, to our surprise, we felt the Lord prompting us to move out of the house we had bought. So we rented it out, moved to where we thought God wanted us to be, and discovered rent-vesting by accident.

It was in my mid-30s that I reached a milestone fifteen years in the making. I received my calling to ministry in 2004. After two degrees — including a second Graduate Diploma of Divinity—and countless other requirements, I was finally accredited as a Baptist Minister through the Baptist Association of NSW & ACT. Not long after, our church plant became an Affiliated Baptist Church. Both felt less like achievements and more like affirmations of what God had already been doing, but nonetheless, they felt great!

In my late 30s, I invested in crypto. It revived my love for macroeconomics and taught me to read charts — but only after I had made every mistake possible. I bought on the way up and held on the way down. I tried to catch the bottom only to watch it fall further. I put too little in when I was right and didn't sell enough when I had every opportunity. The best decisions I made were the most boring ones. We made money but did not beat the market had we just invested into index funds — nonetheless I learnt a lot so it was very much worth it.

In my 40s. Where we are financially, we didn't plan — we discovered God's plan along the way. I can testify that his plans are praiseworthy and his ways are perfect. That is why I wrote this book.

BIBLIOGRAPHY

SELECT BIBLIOGRAPHY & RECOMMENDED RESOURCES

A note on these resources: the following list represents the shoulders of giants upon which this work stands. I have curated these voices because they represent a holistic view of stewardship — spanning the soul, the mind, the body, and the wallet. These are resources I can personally vouch for and that offer a robust foundation for the themes explored in these chapters.

WHAT MONEY ACTUALLY IS

Lapin, D., & Lapin, S. (2023). *Business Secrets from the Bible: Spiritual Success Strategies for Financial Abundance* (2nd ed.). Wiley. Lapin transformed my view of money. If Outlive is the go-to book for health, this is the go-to book for wealth.

Digital Resource: @AndreiJikh on YouTube. Does a great job of helping the everyday person understand economic jargon.

FOLLOW THE MONEY

Kiyosaki, R. T. (1997). *Rich Dad Poor Dad.* Warner Business. Included for the foundational definitions of assets versus liabilities. It provides easy to understand illustrations for modern financial literacy.

THE TITHE

Alcorn, R. (2001). *The Treasure Principle.* Multnomah. Reframes the believer as a temporary steward rather than an owner. Essential for breaking the power of materialism.

THE ART OF WORK

Fraser, R. (2004). *Marketplace Christianity.* New Wine Press. Provides the high-level kingdom vision, giving theological permission to excel in the marketplace as a primary mission field.

Martin, K. (2017). *Workship.* Graceworks. The bridge for the Australian context. Provides the practical how-to for integrating Sunday worship with Monday's work.

Traeger, S., & Gilbert, G. (2013). *The Gospel at Work.* Zondervan. The definitive guardrail against the twin traps of idolatry — making work your god — and idleness — treating work as meaningless.

WORK IN THE REAL WORLD

No additional resources — the principles in this chapter are drawn from scripture, personal observations and experience.

THE SABBATH

Peterson, E. H. (2011). *The Pastor: A Memoir.* HarperOne. Essential for the "bastard Sabbath" concept. This book provides the heart behind the emphasis on identity over productivity.

CLOSE TO HOME

Tyson, J. (2021). *The Intentional Father.* Baker Books. Provides a proactive vision for investing in milestones and memories rather than just accumulating possessions.

Locke, J. (2015). *The Bonsai Child: Why modern parenting limits children's potential and practical strategies to turn it around.* Judith Locke. Locke's research shows that doing too much for children and giving too much to them produces the opposite of what parents intend. A sharp corrective for any parent who equates generosity with good parenting.

HOLD IT LOOSELY

Housel, M. (2020). *The Psychology of Money.* Harriman House. Essential for understanding the behavioural traps of greed and envy. It anchors the definition of enough.

Attia, P. (2023). *Outlive.* Harmony/Rodale. Informs us of the four horsemen that cause preventable death and reframes longevity not by age but by quality of life in later life.

Digital Resource: Yuka app (yuka.io). An ingredient scanning app that flags high-risk chemicals in food and personal care products. Worth downloading before your next grocery run.

DEBT — MASTER OR SLAVE?

No additional resources — the principles in this chapter are drawn from scripture, personal observations and experience.

MASSIVE COMMITMENTS

Lapin, D. (2014). *Thou Shall Prosper.* John Wiley & Sons. Reframes business as a moral act of service. Lapin connects ancient Hebrew wisdom to the mechanics of providing value to others.

MULTIPLY

Graham, B. (1949). *The Intelligent Investor.* Harper Business. The bible of value investing. I include this to introduce the concept of the margin of safety — a principle that is as much about character and humility as it is about stock prices.

Buffett, M., & Clark, D. (1997). *Buffettology.* Scribner. Demystifies the never-sell philosophy and the power of compounding. Provides the technical framework for how a faithful servant manages the talents through business ownership and long-term equity.

JUST LIKE GOD

Corbett, S., & Fikkert, B. (2009). *When Helping Hurts.* Moody. The gold standard for ensuring our generosity restores the person rather than just fixing a temporary financial problem.

LET IT GO

No additional resources — the principles in this chapter are drawn from scripture, personal observations and experience.

SCRIPTURE INDEX

References are listed in canonical order. Each entry is keyed to the relevant chapter of this book.

Genesis

DISCUSSION GUIDE

Thank you for reading The Grip of Money. To help you, your small group, or your church go deeper, download the discussion guide at thegripseries.com.au.

READER NOTES

www.ingramcontent.com/pod-product-compliance
Lightning Source LLC
LaVergne TN
LVHW100317210926
848480LV00003B/1159
9781764708005